Urban Development and Infrastructure

Practical Application of Integrative Rules and Principles of Urban Design

Lessons Learned from the Past

Urban Development and Infrastructure

Additional books and e-books in this series can be found on Nova's website under the Series tab.

URBAN DEVELOPMENT AND INFRASTRUCTURE

PRACTICAL APPLICATION OF INTEGRATIVE RULES AND PRINCIPLES OF URBAN DESIGN

LESSONS LEARNED FROM THE PAST

HOSSEIN BAHRAINY

AND

AMENEH BAKHTIAR

Copyright © 2020 by Nova Science Publishers, Inc.

All rights reserved. No part of this book may be reproduced, stored in a retrieval system or transmitted in any form or by any means: electronic, electrostatic, magnetic, tape, mechanical photocopying, recording or otherwise without the written permission of the Publisher.

We have partnered with Copyright Clearance Center to make it easy for you to obtain permissions to reuse content from this publication. Simply navigate to this publication's page on Nova's website and locate the "Get Permission" button below the title description. This button is linked directly to the title's permission page on copyright.com. Alternatively, you can visit copyright.com and search by title, ISBN, or ISSN.

For further questions about using the service on copyright.com, please contact:
Copyright Clearance Center
Phone: +1-(978) 750-8400   Fax: +1-(978) 750-4470   E-mail: info@copyright.com

NOTICE TO THE READER

The Publisher has taken reasonable care in the preparation of this book, but makes no expressed or implied warranty of any kind and assumes no responsibility for any errors or omissions. No liability is assumed for incidental or consequential damages in connection with or arising out of information contained in this book. The Publisher shall not be liable for any special, consequential, or exemplary damages resulting, in whole or in part, from the readers' use of, or reliance upon, this material. Any parts of this book based on government reports are so indicated and copyright is claimed for those parts to the extent applicable to compilations of such works.

Independent verification should be sought for any data, advice or recommendations contained in this book. In addition, no responsibility is assumed by the Publisher for any injury and/or damage to persons or property arising from any methods, products, instructions, ideas or otherwise contained in this publication.

This publication is designed to provide accurate and authoritative information with regard to the subject matter covered herein. It is sold with the clear understanding that the Publisher is not engaged in rendering legal or any other professional services. If legal or any other expert assistance is required, the services of a competent person should be sought. FROM A DECLARATION OF PARTICIPANTS JOINTLY ADOPTED BY A COMMITTEE OF THE AMERICAN BAR ASSOCIATION AND A COMMITTEE OF PUBLISHERS.

Additional color graphics may be available in the e-book version of this book.

Library of Congress Cataloging-in-Publication Data

ISBN: 978-1-53616-623-1
Library of Congress Control Number: 2019953076

Published by Nova Science Publishers, Inc. † New York

CONTENTS

Preface		vii
Acknowledgment		ix
Introduction		xi
Chapter 1	Why Integrative?	1
Chapter 2	Formulating the Integrative Language of Urban Design	9
Chapter 3	Integrative Rules and Principles of the Language of Urban Design—Conceptual Implications	17
Chapter 4	Theory-Practice Relation in Urban Design	79
Chapter 5	Practical Application of the Urban Design Rules and Principles: Lessons Learned from the Past	89
Summary		153
References		155
About the Authors		169
Index		171
Related Nova Publications		177

PREFACE

Questions have been increasingly raised by academicians, theorists, and professionals concerning the essence, legitimacy, knowledge base and content and especially methods of inquiry of urban design. These questions were dealt with in an original study for almost four decades, the preliminary results, which were published under the title Toward an Integrative Theory of Urban Design (Bahrainy and Bakhtiar, Springer, 2016). The author's premise in that work was that because urban design is a complex and multifaceted field, the most useful theories and methods are ones that are integrative (e.g., substantive: urban space and activities; as well as procedural: integrative rules and principles: artistic-intuitive and scientific-rational). The main purpose of this book is to introduce an integrative method of inquiry for urban design through illustrating the practical application of the proposed urban design rules and principles.

The authors believe this collection will be a great contribution to the understanding and application of the integrative urban design theory and, particularly, its practical rules and principles. This synthesis of theory and practice is expected to prepare thoughtful practitioners in urban design, and therefore, will be of great interest to the professionals, as well as academicians and also the students of urban design, urban planning, architecture, and the art fields.

ACKNOWLEDGMENT

The authors are obliged to express their sincere gratitude to Mr. Thomas P. Charpied for his generous and thoughtful review and editing of our draft manuscript. Although we basically expected Tom a language editing of the text, but, to our surprise, what was actually done was far from our expectation. His constructive comments helped us to clarify some of the critical points in the text to make them easier to understand. This could be attributed to Thomas's deep interest, broad knowledge and enthusiasm. He accepted this commitment at a time he had a very tight work schedule.

Thank you Tom.

INTRODUCTION

Questions have been increasingly raised by academicians, theorists, and professionals concerning the essence, legitimacy, knowledge base, content, theory-practice relation and methods of inquiry of Urban Design. To the extent that, in recent years, some scholars have been debating its status as a discipline and even noting its lack of a widely accepted definition (Cuthbert 2011a) and "a clear role, territory, and authority" (Marshall 2009, 54).

These questions and ambiguities were dealt with in an original study for almost four decades, the preliminary results which were published under the title of *Toward an Integrative Theory of Urban Design* (Bahrainy and Bakhtiar, 2016). Our premise was that since urban design is a complex and multifaceted field, the most useful theories are ones that are integrative (e.g., substantive: urban space and activities; as well as procedural: integrative rules and principles: artistic-intuitive and scientific-rational).

Here, in this book, following a brief discussion on the nature of and justification for "integration," formulation of the Integrative Language of Urban Design will be reviewed, then the Rules and Principles will be described and their conceptual implications will be presented. A major issue in urban planning and particularly in urban design has been the uneasy relation between theory and practice, which even today makes a serious and damaging dichotomy in urban design. The core of the book, therefore, deals with the practical application of the proposed Urban Design rules and principles. This part is done thorough an original analysis of the ancient *Shah (Naghshe Jahan)* Square and its vicinity of the Safavid era (1501 to 1722)—which is the most valuable historical section of the city of Isfahan, Iran. Analysis of these past experiences, which is presented through original drawings, sketches and photos, will support the plausibility of the proposed integrative rules and principles and enable urban designers to imaginatively design future public spaces.

We believe this collection will be a great contribution to the understanding and application of the integrative urban design theory and particularly its practical rules and principles. This synthesis of theory and practice is expected to prepare thoughtful practitioners in urban design and, therefore, will be of great interest to the professionals, as well as academicians and also the students of urban design, urban planning, architecture, and the art fields.

Let's begin with the developments that are taking place in the field of urban planning. In urban planning it is believed that a new paradigm is emerging (Innes, 1995). Contemporary city and urban planning involves three determinant attributes of: complexity, uncertainty and normativity. Sustainability and critical theory are two major contemporary paradigms to deal with these issues. Now, is it possible to merge these two paradigms into a single united paradigm? Why and how?

SUSTAINABILITY introduces an ideal setting (substance or product), without stating how to achieve a good society or good city. It is an attractive, new and exciting idea which was at first presented by a small group but was spread rapidly to other areas. It is heavily ideological in nature and it is appropriate for a society with class and capital. The term "sustainable development" has been used so superficially that has lost its original intended meaning (Campbell, 1996). So that Campbell (1996) who was one of the first experts that gave meaning to the application of sustainable development concept in the urban planning profession questioned its competency to do so. According to him the system we are dealing with is always incomplete and involves unpredictable status. It is, therefore, necessary to find a kind of approach to fit with this ever changing eco-system.

During last 23 years since the publication of "Sustainable Development" article the concept has attracted the attention of urban planners and has been extensively applied in the profession. Its idealistic nature, however, has created serious criticism. So that doubts have been shed on the efficiency and adequacy of the concept, especially in the case of profession. Are we better off today in cities and neighborhoods, compared to three decades ago, many experts ask (Berke, 2016). Campbell (1996) was right when he said "in the fight with great ideas, sustainable development is the winner, but more work is needed in the details to decrease the gap between theory and practice, which requires a complementary theory. This is not a simple task and needs multi-generation efforts.

So, sustainability is a quite valuable concept, puts emphasis on the substance, unification, exciting and innovative, and translatable into resilience. However, it does not pay attention to procedures; it is vague, ideal, not appropriate for implementation, too complex, involves internal paradoxes, and the gap between theory and practice. It is based on closed and controllable system. It needs to be more realistic and practical. For example, instead of creating balance between social, environmental and economic preferences as the basic principles of sustainability, we need to talk about compatibility and a temporary agreement. Such a manageable tension can better adjust itself to the internal paradoxes of urban planning which often draws it to different directions. What sustainability needs is to pay attention to the systems management under the uncertainty conditions.

CRITICAL THEORY, which has been suggested by some (Innes, 1995) as a "paradigm shift" maintains that the political communities may organize to achieve the quality of their community. It is a framework for understanding and practical action, interested in democratic management and the control of urban and regional environments and the design of less oppressed (popular) planning mechanisms. Here the emphasis is on process, not product. In other words, critical theory proposes a procedural approach to deal with problems and how to solve problems, rather than finding solutions. Public domain is a place for political life, civil participation and promoting awareness and social responsibility. Innes (1995) calls this development an "emerging paradigm." Decentralization, challenging beaurocracy, and empowering people and communities in order to, at least, enable them to decide for their future: their life style, culture, and identity, which are among the most important political issues of today. The whole idea is bottom-up political process, considering long-term priorities against short-term ones, based on right ecological principles, and better understanding of the roles of power, dominance, and exploitation in society. So while critical theory puts emphasis on procedure and method, the synthesis of knowledge and dominance of dichotomy, pluralism, emancipation, collective governance, collaboration, dialogue, and pragmatism, it fails to deal with substance. Critical theory rejects the status quo, requires evaluation, is based on human emancipation and leads to a new theory of knowledge which is based on synthesizing knowledge, and thereby overcoming dichotomies, particularly between theory and practice.

The new paradigm pays attention simultaneously to process and product, bottom-up decision-making, using various methods and tools, long-term goals, combining two diverse ways of thinking: divergence and convergence, decentralization and power sharing by people. It Isa good response for complexity (clumsiness) and uncertainty, a framework to think globally and act locally, and finally a bridge between knowledge and decision-making. Combining sustainability with critical theory implies participatory democracy which will eventually lead to a better life and the securing of human needs for all.

As for urban design, several authors have suggested some kind of integration, although with different terminologies, in the urban design theories. Inam (2011) uses the term "From Dichotomy to Dialectic"; Moudon (2003) uses "A Catholic approach"; and Sternberg (2000) suggests "Integrative design." None of these, however, have gone further to explain how this could actually happen and how the suggested theory may be translated into practice. This book intends to overcome this shortcoming.

Introduction

Urban design has been proposed before (see Bahrainy and Bakhtiar 2016, pp vii-vii), as the application of the integrative rules and principles (as grammar) to substantive elements (as vocabulary) in order to establish order in the physical environment (see also Alexander, 2002). This may be considered as a plausible approach to develop a general theory for urban design (Figures 1 and 2).

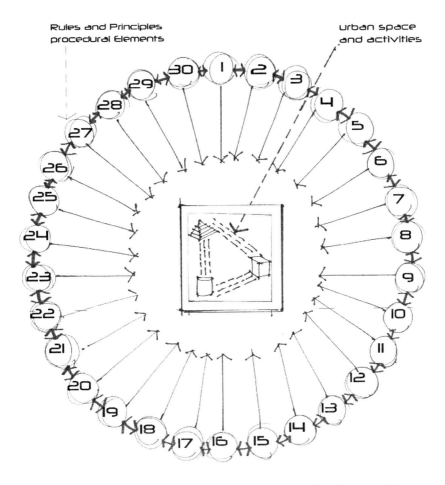

Figure 1. The interrelationship of the procedural and substantive elements of the language of urban design.

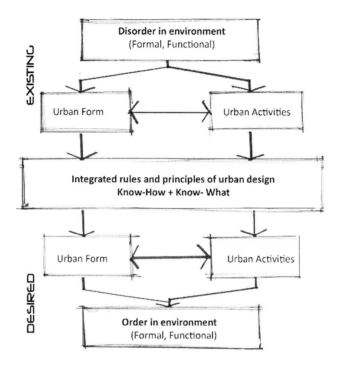

Figure 2. Integrated rules are applied to the disordered environment, manipulating its elements to establish order.

To illustrate the implication of the proposed theory and the application of the proposed principles in a real world situation, Appendix I was added to the end of the Book (Bahrainy and Bakhtiar, 2016). In Appendix I, practical implications of the proposed language and theory of urban design are shown. The purpose of this book is to show how those principles and rules mentioned as the components of the integrative theory of urban design may be applied in the practice of urban design. Several of those rules are frequently used by practicing urban designers, others, however, are not quite known to them.

This is done through an original documentation and analysis of the ancient *Shah (Naghshe Jahan)* Square and its vicinity of the Safavid era (1501 to 1722) in Isfahan, and on the basis of rules and principles that have been proposed before (see Bahrainy and Bakhtiar, 2016, chapter 4). This is believed to be a great contribution to the understanding and application of the integrative theory and its principles of urban design. The case study is focused on a real-world application of the proposed urban design principles, in the most valuable historical section of the city of Isfahan, Iran. No doubt, it will be of great interest to professionals, as well as academicians and students of urban design, urban planning, architecture, art fields, etc.

But first a short discussion on the nature and role of the integrative rules and principles seems necessary. Since 1980's the urban planning field witnessed changes toward integrating and synthesizing knowledge, and thereby overcoming dichotomies in many aspects, particularly the dichotomy between theory and practice. Integrative knowledge is represented through integrative language, on its basis which integrative rules and principles will be formulated.

Over the past decade, planning theorists have used communicative action to understand planning and suggest new approaches to practice. The focus on a communicative basis for planning reflects an inclusive idea of reason that extends beyond analytic methods. A shift, Euclidian toward the non-Euclidian thought, in philosophy led to the creation of phenomenology, sustainability, normative ethical theories, linguistic approach, just city, collaborative planning and design, practical/practice movement, and pragmatism.

Phenomenology is one of those philosophical ideas that have great potential for the theory and practice in all environmental design fields. Phenomenology of environment deals with the man-environment relation, what the environment means to people, or the meaning of space. Phenomenology is defined as the descriptive analysis of subjective processes. It deals with inner perception and is common-sense knowledge. It focuses on the uniqueness of local contexts and knowledge and pays special attention to perception, emotion, and feeling as legitimate sources of knowledge. This is especially an important task at a time when planners are so concerned with substantive paradigms such as Smart Growth, Ecological Sustainability, or the New Urbanism, which each assert their own dominatory narratives. Urban planning theorists have tried to translate those meta-theories into applied theory to be applicable in the practice of urban planning and design. However, there has been very little real-world application of those theories to test and verify their proficiency in practice. This is in fact the main purpose of this book. Through an epistemological analysis, the nature of urban design, as a discipline and a profession was discussed and elaborated, and by taking a linguistic approach, the integrative theory, language and rules and principles of urban design were introduced (see Bahrainy and Bakhtiar, 2016). Theory building in urban planning and design is possible in three ways (see Figure 3): one is through translating the philosophical ideas (meta-theories) into applied theories, second is by extracting rules and principles from the context or field and formulating them into a theory, and the third is the combination of one and two. As it is shown in next pages, critical theory has gone through these phases to turn the philosophical ideas into several interrelated applied theories. In "Toward an integrative theory of urban design" book (ibid) the philosophical-theoretical part was dealt with by using linguistics as a meta theory and by developing the language, theory and rules and principles of urban design, but here the focus will be on the context and the test of the validity of those findings in a real-world situation. Extracting the proposed urban design rules and principles from a real urban design project will support the validity of the proposed rules and principles (see chapter four).

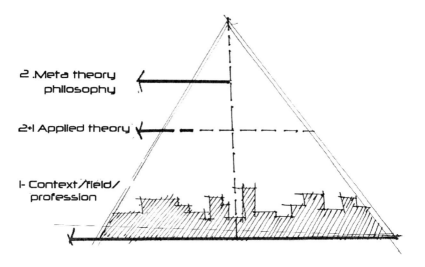

Figure 3. Three ways of formulating the integrative theory of urban design.

Chapter 1

WHY INTEGRATIVE?

Henry Margenau (1972) has edited a comprehensive book entitled *Integrative Principles of Modern Thought* in which various aspects of integration such as: "Integrative Principles of Modern Physics; Quantization as an Integrative Concept; Integrative Principles of Biology; Integrative Principles in Human Society; Integrative Principles of Art and Science and Integrative Concepts in the Logic of Relations", are explained. Half a century has passed since this statement by Margenau. Today almost all contemporary planning and design theories strongly support the idea of the end of dichotomies and the emergence of integration and dualism vs. duality. Even today urban design and planning theories have a diverse and fragmented landscape.

There are many aspects of duality in nature. Some of the more familiar are positive and negative electrical charges, north and south magnetic poles, male and female sexes, and the two directions of electron spin (Margenau, 1972). There have been numerous examples of duality in Urban Design, as follows:

- Artistic vs. scientific
- Science vs. reform
- Advisory vs. active

- Reformist vs. rationalist
- Physical vs. aphysical/anti-physical
- Process vs. product
- Substantive vs. Procedural
- Euclidian vs. Non-Euclidian
- Profession vs. discipline
- Generic vs. specific/specialized
- Partial vs. comprehensive, integrative
- Theory vs. practice
- Consensus vs. control
- Science vs. humanity
- Continuity vs. discontinuity

For over half a century there has been serious debate by academicians in urban planning on the possibility of formulating a general and coherent planning theory. In 1960's Briton Harris, for example, claimed that "A general model for city and city planning" was possible. However, Mandelbaum (1979) rejected this idea by stating that "A complete general theory of planning is impossible." Mandelbaum argued against the possibility of a complete general theory of planning, while Donaghy and Hopkins (2006) suggest a coherentist approach to planning theories that achieves some of the aspirations Mandelbaum sought for a general theory.

Also, John Friedmann suggested in "Quest for a General Theory of Planning" that a new way of thinking about planning was needed that would emphasize the relationship between knowledge and action. These ideas shifted the discourses of planning away from planning as an instrument of control to one of innovation and action. (Friedmann, 2003: 8). Antonio Ferreira (2018) tries to bring Wilber's philosophy to planning theory and practice by suggesting an integrative perspective. Rittel and Webber (1973) in a very interesting article, which discusses the dilemma a general theory of planning is facing, states that the idea of a single universal paradigm of planning as the model for a general theory of planning is not in the agenda. They, instead, suggest a contingent framework, which offers the possibility of developing a general theory of planning to integrate various seemingly incompatible and diverse theories and models. A general framework for understanding planning as a dynamic process which can take a variety of forms, depending on particular contingencies: the ideal (normative, analytical), the real (empirical, descriptive); contextual dimensions: culture, norms, politics; economic and institutional frameworks; aspects of planning systems and professional issues, problems, and characteristics.

Ferreira, Sykes, & Batey (2009) suggest four different views of a contingent framework for integrative planning theory, or what they call "planning theory," instead of planning theories:

1. Planning as deliberative
2. Planning as interactive
3. Planning as coordinative
4. Planning as frame setting

In the case of functional issues such as transportation, Hull (2008) believes that policy integration will achieve more sustainable transport solutions in cities. And Sydow (2018) claims that dualities, rather than dualism, will lead to creative processes in the arts and sciences (see Figure 4).

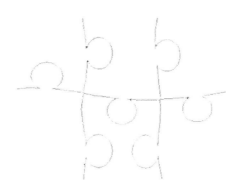

Figure 4. How duality turns into dualism—integration.

CRITICAL THEORY is one of the significant meta-theories that has been successfully transformed and evolved into applied theory, and thereby into practical methods (see the next few diagrams).

EVOLUTION OF CRITICAL THEORY: FROM PHILOSOPHICAL IDEAS TO APPLIED THEORIES

CRITICAL THEORY

COMMUNICATIVE ACTION

COLLABORATIVE PLANNING

PRAGMATIVE PLANNING/PRAGMATIVE COMMUNICATIVE ACTION
Charles Sanders Peirce in1878, William James, John Dewey, George Herbert Mead, George Santayana, Clarence Lewis, Richard Rorty, Hillary Putnam, Richard Bernstein, Hans Joas, Charlene Seigfried and Charles Hoch

past experience enables us to imaginatively project likely futures, and, therefore to plan using an emphasis on experience rather than on abstracted theory; a rejection of the dichotomies of modern science and philosophy, for example, belief/action, theory/practice, facts/values, intellect/emotion; the centrality of community and social relationships; and a recognition of the importance of language in creating realities and in shaping social practice

PRACTICAL/PRACTICE MOVEMENT

DIALOGICAL PLANNING PROCESS: MANTYSALO'S

+

FALUDI

+

DAVIDSON'S AND RORTY'S FLEXIBLE APPROACH TO COMMUNICATIVE INTERPRETATION

(Rejects traditional view of language)
(Fluidity of language)
DIALOGUE
(A dialogical approach to communication)

RAWL'S

+

WIDE REFLECTIVE EQUILIBRIUM

+

TWO KINDS OF THINKING

DIVERGENCE	CONVERGENCE
INNOVATION	CREATIVITY
PERFORMANCE	CONFORMANCE

So, as Raelin (2007) has stated, if we are to prepare thoughtful practitioners, we need a synthesis of theory and practice.

As for urban design, a conventional assumption about theory and practice is that they represent a dichotomy in which theory represents abstract thinking to explain observations, while practice depends on a more instrumental conception of knowledge to help accomplish tasks. Effort is made here to examine this dichotomy under the premise that urban design is primarily an intellectual activity, and that the theory/practice relationship can take a number of mutually beneficial forms, especially when it is dialectical. Furthermore, the paper suggests that since urban design is a complex and multifaceted field, the most useful theories are ones that are integrative (i.e., that incorporate function, form and process) rather than singular (e.g., based almost exclusively on ideas of green design, technology or historicism). These ideas were tested in an experimental urban design studio for graduate students at the Massachusetts Institute of Technology in 2009. The paper introduces the theory being applied, Kevin Lynch's book Good City Form, describes the pedagogical process as an investigation of the theory/practice relationship, and concludes with insights for professional practice.

Davoudi and Pendlebury (2010: 638), in their attempt to define the 'epistemic core' of the 'planning discipline,' focus on 'space as the discipline's substantive object of inquiry,' on the particular integrative approach to knowledge development and use, and on the close connection between knowledge and action.

Human experience is rich and varied and amenable to treatment in many different ways. Recent trends in philosophy have emphasized one aspect of it –the cognitive one– and tended to disregard the rest. Positivism has sought to reduce everything meaningful in experience to the elements which go into the making of natural science. These elements are important, and their share in our total experience grows as science succeeds in organizing them. But as Margenau (1972) points out, although we expect the domain of cognitive experience to grow, perhaps to grow forever, there is no indication at all that it will someday embrace all of human experience.

Recognition of the rich and varied ground of experience means that we must view science as one, among many, modes of organizing and comprehending our experience. It means that a large segment of our experience remains forever beyond the scope of science, not beyond that of our comprehension. For we deal with the necessarily non-scientific components of experience, the rich world of feelings, in a manner that leads to specific modes of comprehension, different from that of science but no less illuminating. Art is one way to organize and comprehend our feelings as significant; religion is another. Neither will be taken over by science as we know it, for science cannot correlate theoretical constructs with data as nebulous as feelings. But art and religion can do it, to judge from the historical record, they can do it most successfully.

Limitations of the positivistic reduction to represent all meaningful experience and also the metaphysical or ideological ones to cover the entire field of experience are quite well-known. So we can find integrative principles by means of which human experience can be fully and consistently encompassed. To integrate different diverse worlds (e.g., scientific and artistic) consistently we must resort to a meta-level theory for integration.

Urban design seeks not to eliminate the planning and design professions but to integrate them and in so doing, to go beyond each one's charter (Vernez-Moudon 1992, p. 362). Moudon (1992) suggests "A Catholic approach to organizing what urban designers should know," Catholic in a generic sense of the word, means broad in sympathies, tastes, and interests. Being catholic is not to be partisan, but rather nonsectarian, tolerant of and open to different approaches. Hence the body of knowledge surveyed herein comes from various fields and disciplines allied to urban design that, together, laid the ground work for an epistemology for urban design. Moudon, however, acknowledges that procedural research is not included in this epistemological map and she has only covered the substantive aspects of urban design, disregarding the procedural aspects. According to Lang (1987), there is also research pertaining to the procedural aspects of urban design that relates to how urban design should be practiced and that focuses on methods of practicing urban design, for example see: Barnett (1974), Jacobs (1978), Wolfe and Shinn (1970), Shirvani (1985) and Bahrainy (1998).

Abukhater (2009) presents an agenda for building a new integrative approach to planning, discusses major issues that planning theorists need to address in terms of functional integration, decision-making processes in planning, and political and institutional challenges to such integrated planning approaches, and offers a series of propositions to remedy these challenges. The adaptive sustainable planning model is suggested and amply delineated as an effective overarching normative framework for the development of an integrated planning approach that provides organization to the field and guides practitioners towards realizing their role as effective decision makers.

Chapter 2

FORMULATING THE INTEGRATIVE LANGUAGE OF URBAN DESIGN

A reflective awareness of the way that communication actually works, and of the fluid nature of language, will help the planner to foster creativity and innovation. If she views language, concepts, meanings, and beliefs as fluid, dynamic, and flexible, her interpretation of planning language will be more adaptable to changing environments. She can better generate and adapt new ideas, new ways of framing problems, and new ways of meeting goals.

Edward O. Wilson (1999) has used the term consilience as the key to unification, or unity of knowledge and Henry Margenau (1972) has proposed the Integrative Principles of Modern Thought. In Chapter Three of this book Donald H. Andrews looks at quantization as an integrative concept.

William Whewell, in his 1840 Synthesis of the Philosophy of the Inductive Sciences, was the first to speak of consilience, literally "a jumping together" of knowledge by the linking of facts and fact-based theory across disciplines to create a common ground work of explanation (in: Wilson, 1999, p. 8).

The general guidelines outlined before (Bahrainy and Bakhtiar, 2016) will be used in the formulation of the language of urban design. Among these, the requirements and qualifications mentioned in points five and six are critically important. Still more important are the signs and their qualifications, since they represent the substance of the knowledge base of urban design. The knowledge base of urban design, as suggested above, is an integrated, complex knowledge consisting of intuitive-scientific procedural elements and formal-functional substantive elements. The language of urban design as a method of communication and a symbolic and representation tool, should represent all the individual components of the knowledge base of urban design; its attributes and points of focus as well as the overall complexity, unity and interrelationship of the various aspects of the knowledge base. In order to qualify as a language, these factors must be reflected in the two basic elements of the language devised.

We now proceed to construct the language of urban design by exploring the equivalent of the two language elements and by testing them against the five criteria adopted earlier. The two basic requirements are: A vocabulary, or a set of signs, and a grammar, or a set of rules.

To fill the significant roles of representation and communication efficiently and properly, the signs of the language must be common signs, i.e., their meanings and interpretations must be shared by all the parties involved. To achieve this goal, the language of urban design must include both the language of the physical environment– formal and functional– as well as the procedural language which deals with the process of design itself. The formal language of the environment deals with space, form, perception and vision; the functional language is concerned with the content of urban form, with the activities that take place in the urban environment.

From the four areas of the knowledge base of urban design, substantive elements are equivalent to the vocabulary or signs and procedural elements are equivalent to the grammar or rules of the language. Vocabulary, therefore, will represent the element of (1) urban form and space, and the element of (2) urban activities. Rules, on the other hand, will represent the integrative, intuitive and scientific principles applied in urban design (see Figure 5).

Formulating the Integrative Language of Urban Design

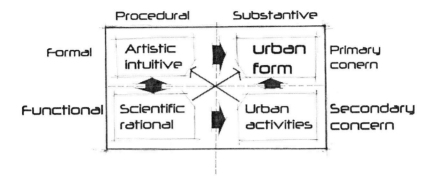

Figure 5. The interrelationship of the procedural and substantive elements of the language of urban design.

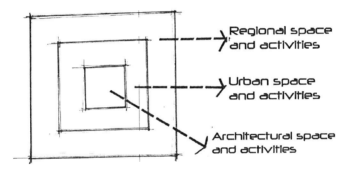

Figure 6. Hierarchical relationship of the substantive elements in three areas of environmental design.

Signs, which represent the substantive elements of knowledge are to be the smallest complete and meaningful units (such as words in a spoken language), which can be combined with other units, according to certain rules, to form larger structures (such as sentences). As mentioned above, it is absolutely essential for these signs to thoroughly represent the substantive elements of urban design. To do this, they have to be defined exclusively and inclusively in order to be differentiated from similar signs which represent other areas such as architectural and regional spaces and activities, which, although they maintain a reciprocal and hierarchical relationship with urban space and activities, contain a different level of complexity and size which represent different areas of environmental design (see Figure 6).

The smallest complete unit of urban form is *urban space*. Urban space has been under broad investigation by many researchers and writers, due to its determining role in urban design (see for example: Ross King, G. Broadbent, Christoph Lindner; Stephan Carr, Mark Francis, Leanne G. Rivlin and Andrew M. Stone; Rob Krier, Matthew Carmona, Geoffrey Broadbent, John Morris Dixon, Mike Crang, Tridib Banerjee, etc.).

Urban space is defined here as the container of the average daily circuit which is composed of urban activity systems. The aggregate of the daily circuit of urban activity systems, which represents the smallest complete unit of urban activities in the language of urban design is defined here as the average of a person's daily, weekly or yearly routine activities in the urban environment. These activities include such things as recreational activities, shopping, driving to work, going to a place of worship walking to school, visiting, etc. Repetitive patterns of such activities are called *urban activity patterns*, examples of which are: shopping patterns, home to work commuting patterns, recreational patterns, and so on (Figures 7 and 8).

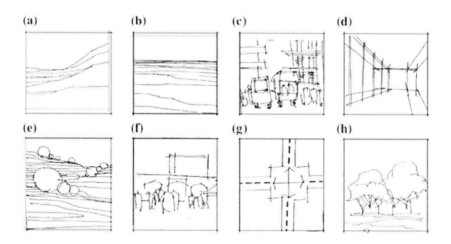

Figure 7. Examples of urban spaces a–c: different urban destinations.

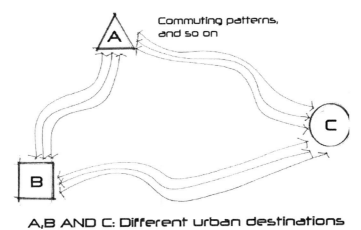

Figure 8. Urban activity patterns.

Urban space and the *circuit of urban activities* which represent urban form and urban activity systems correspondingly, comprise the signs or units, or the vocabulary of the urban design language; these satisfy the rest requirement for a language of urban design. It should be pointed out that urban space is static by nature as is each activity in its own particular location. The relationship between the activities, however, is dynamic and creates movement in the urban environment.

This occurs because of the spatial distribution of activities in the environment which may be represented by the distance between the activities or its proxy in time. This factor is the basis of the circuit of activities.

As mentioned earlier, the two units—urban space and activity circuit—have to meet certain requirements in order to qualify as the signs of the language. To this end, they will be tested here against the five criteria adopted earlier. This test has, of course, only a general validity because it does not consider the cultural differences in the meaning and interpretation of these signs. The resultant language of urban design will obviously require a great deal of modification of the signs.

First, the plurality of signs criteria is met here because each set of signs may be repeated numerous times. An activity circuit is the unit of urban activity systems; it is what people do in the urban environment. The repetition of an activity circuit leads to an urban activity pattern. The unit of urban space is also repeatable and its repetition leads to a larger physical environment.

Second, the significations of the signs are shared by the users and participants. Since the units represent the activities people engage in and the space in which these activities take place, their significations are shared by the participants.

Third, the signs are producible by the participants and users, and when produced will convey a common meaning. Producibility is in fact, the result of the two previous elements of plurality and the common signification of signs. In other words, when signs have the characteristics of plurality, they are producible; when they have common significations, the produced signs will convey a common signification.

Fourth, the signs have a relatively constant signification. The units of urban space and the activity circuit do not belong to any specific environment. Rather, they are abstract and their significations, therefore, are also universal. The signs simply represent the urban physical environment. Although one may see many similarities between the various daily activities of the inhabitants of different cultures, what is more critical and valuable are the dissimilarities and differences between the units in different places and different times. Some of these differences have been already investigated cross-culturally (examples are the meanings and uses of spaces). The meanings and significations of signs, therefore, are culturally bound and also subject to significant changes (Bahrainy 1995).

Finally, signs are combinable on the basis of certain rules. In the case of language of urban design, these are the integrative rules and principles of the discipline. These integrative rules and principles satisfy the second requirement for a language of urban design. The idea behind searching for the units and constructing the language is to eventually control and guide the formation of the larger structures on the basis of certain general rules and principles. In other words, in order to achieve certain desired goals in the physical environment, the process of building the environment has to be based on these rules and principles. These rules govern the relationship between nature and the built environment, between man and the environment and between man and man himself.

To qualify as the rules of language of urban design, the rules must: thoroughly represent the procedural elements of the knowledge base of urban design, which is the application of the integrative-intuitive and scientific methods in urban design (elements 3 and 4), and (2) have the capacity to construct larger structures out of the units (urban space and activities); these larger structures must fit the general characteristics and qualifications of the signs or units that were given before (see Figure 5). This set of criteria requires that the rules of the language be derived from or based on the contents and characteristics of the substantive elements of urban design, i.e., on urban form and urban activity systems. Efforts, therefore, have been made to explore a set of rules and principles which can best represent the complexity and diversity of the methods and processes applied in urban design.

Chapter 3

INTEGRATIVE RULES AND PRINCIPLES OF THE LANGUAGE OF URBAN DESIGN— CONCEPTUAL IMPLICATIONS

Art and science are both necessary and should exist, but both need significant integration if we are to succeed in specific and coordinated urban design knowledge (Cuthbert 2007).

Procedural rules are carefully extracted from a variety of concepts, principles, theories and rules which have been commonly applied in urban design or which have the potential of being commonly applied in the future. Again, the aspect of commonality should be emphasized here because it is essential for the formulation of a common language. As a real representation of the integrated methods and processes of urban design, these rules and principles must also be integrated into a unified set of rules and principles. The integration of these rules, however, should be considered a mental activity which may be realized through intuition. The successful application of the language of urban design is heavily dependent on such an intuitive integration of these rules.

There are three points to be explained here with regard to these rules and principles. First, this list is not to be considered a complete and exhaustive one. There may be some principles which have not been included and others that have yet to be developed. Second, the principles are derived from three different sources of knowledge (see Figure 9): 1) From the available relevant meta-theories (or philosophy), such as critical theory, sustainability, normative ethical theories, linguistics, etc.; 2) from the field or the practice of urban design; 3) from the combination of 1 and 2. Third, the principles should not be seen as independent and complete in and of themselves. They are interrelated and interdependent members of the family of the language of urban design. This language represents the integrated knowledge base of urban design (Figures 10 and 11).

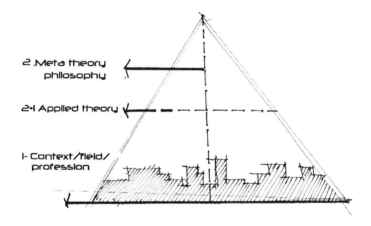

Figure 9. Three ways of formulating the integrative theory of urban design.

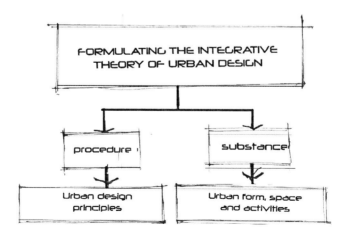

Figure 10. Formulating the language (theory) of urban design.

Integrative Rules and Principles of the Language of Urban Design 19

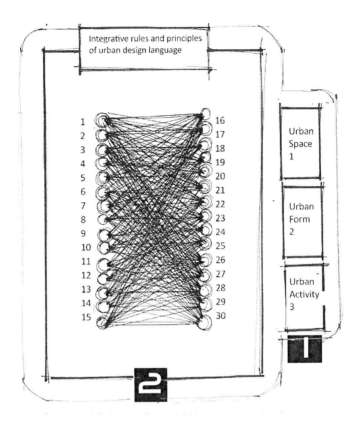

Figure 11. Integrative rules and principles of urban design language.

Fourth, based on what was suggested before, the activities of urban design may be on two levels: global and local. In many cases, however, due to some common characteristics— such as religious, socio-economic, and climatic conditions in certain regions, one more level may be recognized as regional. The local level is in fact the culture specific one and best fits the unique characteristics of each settlement or a group of settlements. The following rules and principles are presented in two categories: global and local. For local, we used the cities in the hot and dry region on the central plateau of Iran, which includes the cities of Isfahan, Yazd, Kashan, etc.

PATTERNIZATION

An orderly repetition of a form, event or state is a pattern and an orderly repetition of a pattern is patternization. This general and broad definition covers many different kinds of patterns which are all of basic significance in the activities of man and hence, in the field of urban design (Figures 12a and 12b).

Patterns and patternization are essential to the functioning of all the human senses and to the human intellect. They are the basis of human senses and human perception, knowing and understanding: seeing, hearing, and perceiving. Patternization portrays movement and causes a visual dynamism. So a pattern or motif could create predictability, order, rhythm and harmony in a place that is influenced by, inspired by and impacted by human perception, and vice versa. Actually, repetition of using the same element in design is used by the designer to attract viewers' attentions to the repeated element and create a visual echo that reinforces certain aspects of the design to infuse a specific sense that increases or decreases special behaviors, reactions or manners in the place (induction of movement in the bazaar by repeating the catching of natural light, or inducing a sense of both stasis and movement through repetition of open and close in the form of semi-open arches on a historic bridge). So this purpose could be accomplished by a basic design element or alphabet, or vocabulary, in each context and culture, which most people communicate with based on their identity and history. It can illustrate a multisensory aesthetic. Patternization is the mother principle in a way that all other principles are by their nature, in one way or another, related to this principle, which is due to its relevance to the foundation of human intellect.

Here are examples explaining the rules applied for creation of rhythm, which are categorized by the nature of the repetition:

1. *Repetition in form (regular)*: A regular rhythm is created by repeating an element through regular recurrence; the repeated elements are often similar.

Integrative Rules and Principles of the Language of Urban Design 21

2. *Repetition in structure (structure)*: A structure rhythm is created by similar structural elements in size or dimensions that maintain the structural properties of equilibrium.
3. *Repetition in lights (reflective)*: A reflective rhythm is created by opening up a surface with a repeated regular module to let light in. The shadows cast on walls will also create a reflective rhythm.
4. *Repetition in functions (spatial)*: A spatial rhythm is created when module spaces recur to accommodate similar or repetitive functional requirements in program.
5. *Repetition in movement (flowing)*: Provides a motion of movement and is organic in nature (Mc Clurg-Genevese, 2005).
6. *Repetition in process (iterative)*: Could be generated not only by regular recurrence of an element, but also by iteration to create a comfortable visual result.
7. *Repetition in growth (progressive)*: Rhythm can also be created by reverberating a shape or a form from a point and additively growing it in a certain direction or following a certain path (Ching, 1979). (Chan, 2012).

They have been the subjects of extensive scientific study under the heading of invariance. A special form of invariance is called symmetry. Symmetry is so prevalent that we expect a certain degree of symmetry in everything. In addition, human minds are taught to look for patterns and symmetry in the environment. Symmetry signifies rest and binding, while asymmetry signifies motion and loosening. One is order and law, the other arbitrariness and accident. The one represents formality, rigidity, constraint and principle while the other represents life, play and freedom. "A simple way to balance or unify a work of art is through symmetry, the mirrorlike repetition of the two halves of an image or object. Symmetrical structures are compositionally stable" Leonardo da Vinci (Mascia, 2018).

Symmetry establishes a wonderful cousinship between objects, phenomena and theories, which are outwardly unrelated. Philosophers and art historians seem generally agreed that although symmetry is indeed attractive, there is also a somewhat sterile rigidity about it, which can make it less attractive than the more dynamic, less predictable beauty associated with asymmetry. Although a little asymmetry can be beautiful, an excess merely results in chaos. As Adorno suggested, asymmetry probably results most effectively in beauty when the underlying symmetry upon which it is built is still apparent. There is also a suggestion that art develops, with symmetry as a more primitive, simpler form of representation or portrayal which evolves, with all the (non-biological) connotations of progress, into asymmetry (McManus, 2005).

So, it may be said that humans enjoy symmetry in two ways. One is, as stated above, the symmetry is apparent but what is beautiful is how the symmetry interacts with or promotes and relationship with asymmetry. Such as asymmetric use of a bazaar by humans via socio-economic interactions amidst a symmetrically designed bazaar. The other way they enjoy is finding symmetry in the asymmetric. If symmetry is at the forefront of design, it comes across as rigid because it is too apparent and less artfully installed. However, if the object or system being presented is by initial view asymmetric until those symmetries are identified by each individual user it is more beautiful. It almost personalizes the identification of the symmetry for the beholder, as if it was theirs and theirs alone to find, evaluate, and appreciate.

Patternization also deals with simplicity, regularity, stability, balance, order, harmony and homogeneity. A classical exemplification of the law of patternization in urban design is perceptual organization, or the tendency to maximize regularity in our perceptual system.

The urban environment is constituted by patterns, such as patterns of settlements, patterns of ecology, patterns of behavior, patterns of perceptual and visual continuity, the rhythm and pattern of events, sequences of space, views and motions, geometrical forms and patterns such as the central place theory and grid system, the patterns of cities, and so on (Figure 12a and 12b). However, searching and selection of design patterns are the two main issues which can be addressed before the employment of the right pattern in each place.

Integrative Rules and Principles of the Language of Urban Design 23

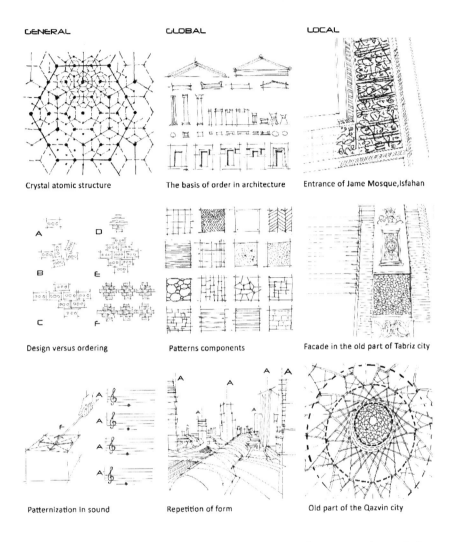

Figure 12a). An orderly repetition of a form, event or state is pattern and an orderly repetition of pattern is patternization.

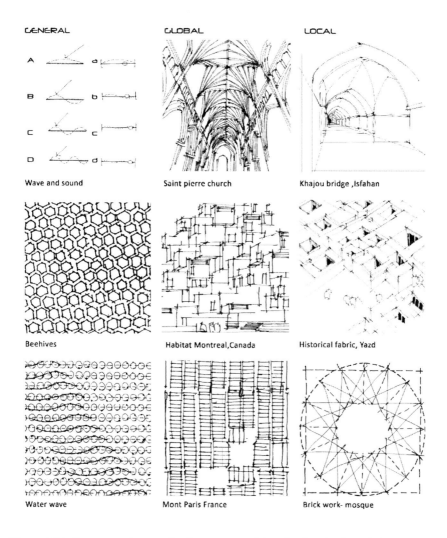

Figure 12b). Patterns and patternization are essential to the functioning of all the human senses and to the human intellect.

QUANTIZATION

Quantization is based on the Quantum Theory (Max Plank 1900) which has the fundamental role in modulation and is one aspect of patternization. It deals with continuity/discontinuity concepts. Its application can be seen in all areas to explain, measure, and control change (visual quality).

Visual characteristics such as attractiveness, complexity, richness, legibility, and cohesion; and how they differ from dullness, simplicity, poorness, boredom, monotony, ambiguity, confusion, chaos, and repetition can be studied analytically through this principle. Desired change and repetition, continuity, balance, movement, diversity, and cohesion may be achieved through measuring visual quality. It is based on the concepts of continuity and discontinuity. In the physical environment one can find complementary aspects of continuity and discontinuity in the form of fluctuations in the level of information. In fact discontinuity is necessary for creating abundant data of city. It links all the elements on the urban level and interestingly makes the whole urban environment continuous. In the structures made of these fluctuations (or waves), there are the complementary aspects of repetition and variation. The bundles of these waves are combined in the total structure to produce organic complexes that are more than the sum of their component parts. The physical environment provides patterns, which follow the quantization rules. These rules will provide new insights into the correlation of ideas and concepts in urban design. Quantization in urban form deals with the visual quality of the built environment and with people's perceptions, preferences and tastes. The quantization principle makes it possible to quantify measure, explain, predict and control the rhythmic changes of the visual quality of the environment. It is the form, size and frequency of these rhythmic changes (waves) that make an environment exciting, complex, rich, legible, identifiable and cohesive or, conversely, boring, monotonous and confusing. In traditional Iranian architecture the continuity of space is understandable as well as the evolution of the world's design, but the continuity in modern architecture, is more visual and physical while the continuation of the space in Iranian architecture is more spiritual. Continuity of signs, their meaning and its connection with their transformation during time is a general principle in eastern societies (Figure 13). (For more information see Chapter 4 & 5).

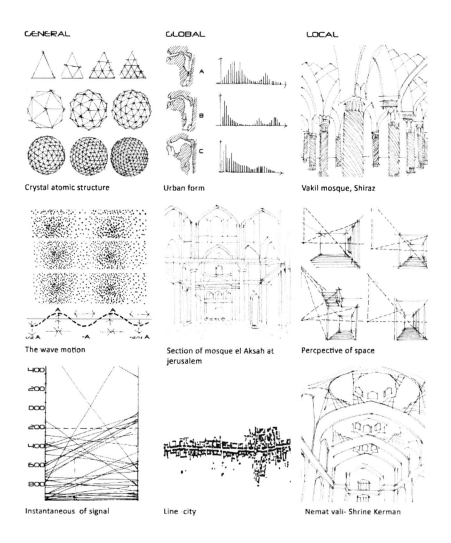

Figure 13. Quantization deals with continuity/discontinuity concepts.

CENTRALITY

Centrality is a very common form of patternization, which can be applied to almost any subject including that of urban design. Many examples of such an application may be found in environmental design for

Integrative Rules and Principles of the Language of Urban Design 27

the urban core, central business district, nodes, commercial centers, inner city, town centers, etc.

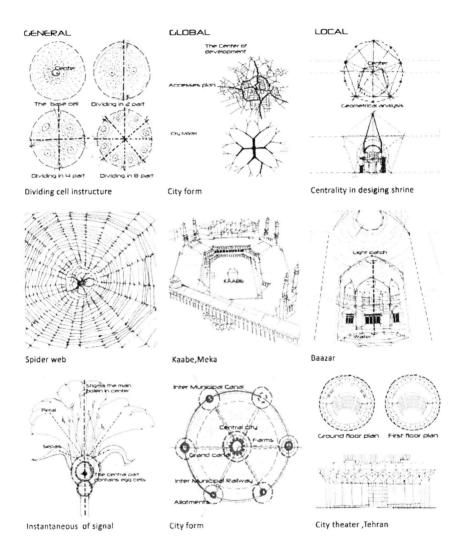

Figure 14a). Centrality is a very common form of patternization.

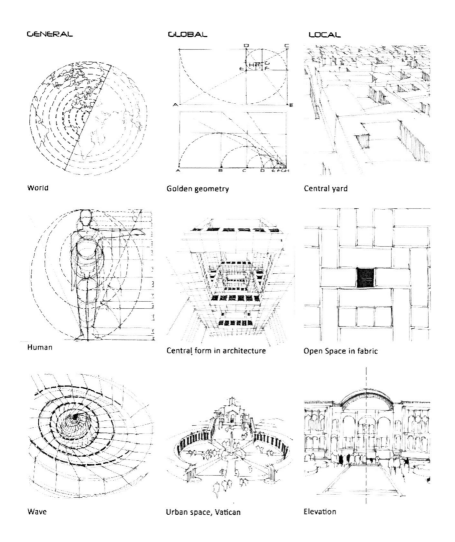

Figure 14b). Centrality in urban design may be said to originate from many sources such as religious impulse, economic forces and cultural and symbolic factors.

Historically, the center of the city has occupied a dominant position. Those have all been perceived as the most prominent urban places, the foci of political, economic, and cultural activity. Most are now symbols of past glories, fading loci of outmoded urban and social processes. In the contemporary city the center is the "downtown," the "heart of the city," the "inner core," the "nucleus," the hub," or, the most importantly, the "central business district." It is usually the major employment center in the region, the locus of most activities of metropolitan importance, the focus of highway and public transport networks, and the place where land values are highest (Polydorides, 1983).

Any urban design activity deals with the patterns of centering, sub-centering, and non-centering as the form expressions of different actions and reactions to the environment. From the market standpoint, for example, it is always possible to apply the central place theory and to identify the central activity cluster within each physically identifiable urban node. However, more sophisticated approaches must be sought to distinguish each center's place in the hierarchy of centers according to the extent of the territorial market establishments that are located there.

It is a basic psychological need to erect centers. This must be considered in the layout and formation of activity centers in cities. This need might manifest itself either in real world centers or in the centers of the inner world. One, however, reflects the need for the other.

Centrality, by organizing elements of design, is one of the solutions for making unity in design. Centrality in urban design may be said to originate from many sources such as religious impulse, economic forces and cultural and symbolic factors. It is said, for example, that if man is to orient himself in the world, he must somewhere erect a fixed point, a center. It seems, therefore, that a centering process is capable of generating wholeness in the three-dimensional constellation of spaces which form a building, a garden, or a street, a neighborhood, and even a city (Figures 14a and 14b).

BOUNDARIES

Related to both quantization and patternization is the presence of boundaries of one kind or another. The undelimited field emphasizes continuity while boundaries emphasize discontinuity. Consequently, systems, which have been described as, bounded regions in space-time with an interchange of energy among their parts; possess boundaries, which may be simple and clear-cut, as in the case of a tree, or nonmaterial. Boundaries define spaces in the physical environment, which will in turn lead to identity, safety, security and freedom.

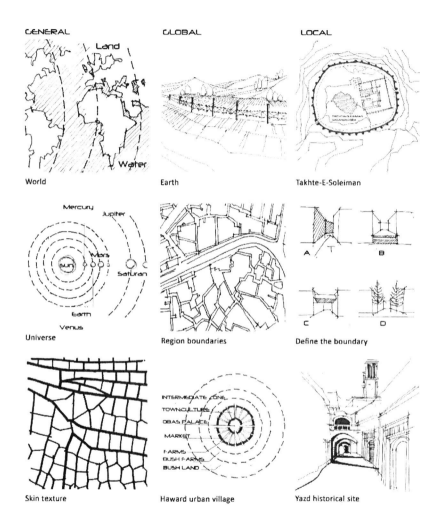

Figure 15. Related to both quantization and patternization is the presence of boundaries of one kind or another.

Boundaries are involved in the making of choices. In the natural landscape, geometrical discontinuities will often provide such boundaries and these physiographical boundaries are retained or directly related to

Integrative Rules and Principles of the Language of Urban Design 31

man's goal-seeking within that environment, and to his technological capabilities to attain such goals.

Boundaries provide diversity of choice and opportunity in the form and function of the environment. Boundaries, either spatial or temporal, make the environment live and dynamic, since they are the source of change and movement. Boundaries in urban form may appear in the form of edges, surfaces, lines, etc. which differentiate two or more different but adjacent urban forms. These differences in urban form can be in density, height, topography, intensity, style, color, materials, relationships or any combination of these and other elements. In the case of perceptual processes, there could be boundaries that might not be tangible or sensible to some observers but which could be sensible and identifiable to others.

Perceptual boundaries, therefore, can be images rather than concrete forms. An optimal combination of these elements in the physical environment results in complexity, diversity and cohesiveness (Figure 15).

TERRITORIES

Territories are also part of the principle of boundaries. They deal with the division of the environment into spatial or temporal regions, symbolically controlled by various individuals or groups, within which certain types of behavior are expected. A simple and familiar example is the division of the environment into private and public spaces.

This principle deals with boundary, borders, domain, realm, sphere, privacy, and sense of belonging, sense of place, possession, ownership, and defensible space. This division could be temporal or spatial, i.e., I world versus others' (it) world. One can also find natural, political, administrative, economic, and functional boundaries in the environment. Some territories are simply visible, while others are only perceptual (invisible). There are various tools in architecture and urban design to define and divide territories, such as walls, fences, doors, gates, etc.

32   *Hossein Bahrainy and Ameneh Bakhtiar*

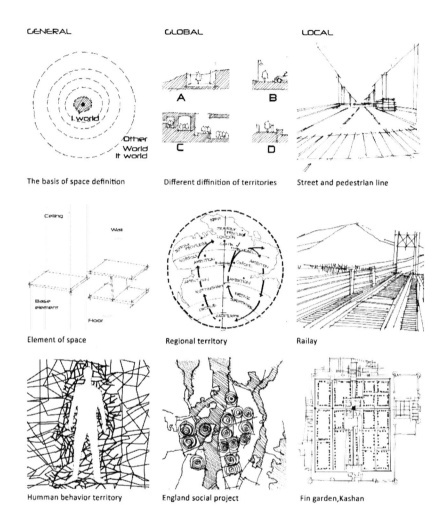

Figure 16a). Territories are also part of the principle of boundaries.

Main characteristics of territories include: Identity, defining and limiting, allocation, defining the role of "self" in space, orientation, cognition, movement, change, diversity/choice, excitement, sense of belonging, sense of possession, familiarity/knowing, safety and security, calm. One of the positive aspects of territories is integration which could take place by: focusing on public realm, public space celebrated, shared spaces, mixed use, externalized facilities, unifying elements, and

Integrative Rules and Principles of the Language of Urban Design 33

integrating neighborhoods (through activity corridors, continuous parks, permeable boundaries, and symbolic borders).

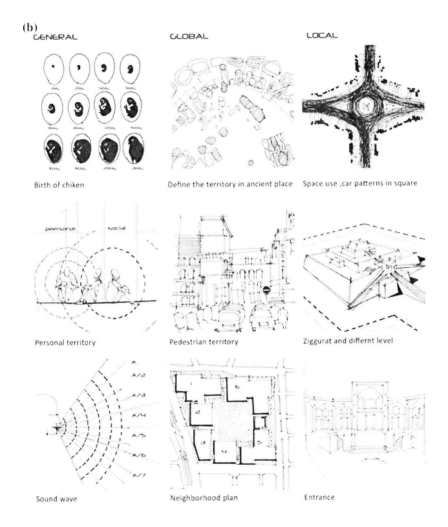

Figure 16b). Territories deal with the division of the environment into spatial or temporal regions.

Territories may also lead to segregation by focusing on private realm, privatization of public space, separation of land uses, separation of neighborhoods, fortification, fortified boundaries, physical borders, special zones, and gated communities.

Man can consciously retain his identity within the perceptual field by imposing physical and/or conceptual boundaries which enable him to differentiate himself as a self-conscious, conceptualizing, being form the external characteristics of his environment. The idea of a territory, therefore, implies the awareness of the self as something unique in an "I" and "IT" world. It relates to the images that man makes for himself of the world, images that are hierarchically ordered according to the degree of closure. The principle of territories provides man in the environment with a sense of identity, orientation, self-awareness, self-direction, imagibility, movement, change, excitement, security, familiarity and so on.

Territoriality in urban form implies that the area which is identified and encircled by its physical, perceptual or visual boundaries, share certain formal, perceptual, visual and aesthetic attributes. These shared elements differentiate one territory from another and give the members of a territory certain privileges such as view, security, prestige, etc. There are also territories, which are identified with intangible and invisible boundaries such as the social group of a neighborhood (Figures 16a and 16b).

BINARY

The binary principle deals with either/or judgments and choices of an extreme nature. Binary oppositions may be temporal, spatial or both. The principle of binary opposition divides the world into two contradictory parts such as inside/outside, good/bad, big/small, round/square, open/closed, simple/complex, symmetrical/ asymmetrical, public/private, dispersed/ condensed, void/full and tall/short.

There is also another binary form which rejects the either/or condition and suggests the both/and form. The basis of this binary form is hierarchy, which yields several levels of meaning among elements with varying values. Some examples of the binary principle in this form are: inside and

Integrative Rules and Principles of the Language of Urban Design 35

outside, simple and complex, round and square, big and small, tall and short, open and closed, wide and narrow, etc.

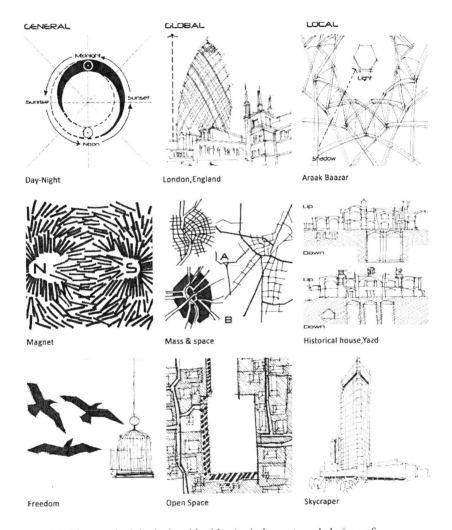

Figure 17. Binary principle deals with either/or judgments and choices of an extreme nature.

The binary principle may be applied to both the functional and formal elements of the urban environment. Binary forms, which contain extreme contrasts of height, size, form or history, might become landmarks.

Functional binary forms, at the extreme level, may result in incompatible uses and activities such as fast traffic versus slow traffic, manufacturing activities versus residential activities, high rise versus single family structures, etc (Figure 17).

Hierarchy

Both/and binary forms are the basis of hierarchy. The notion of hierarchy lies in the nature of very complex and evolving systems. Hierarchical organizations can be usefully applied to the understanding, design and control of complex systems such as the physical environment. In the case of the physical environment the theory of hierarchies is an open one which can continuously grow and evolve to form new levels.

Hierarchical order is the most natural way for ordering dynamic phenomena. It means movement and change, diversity and choice.

It implies putting contracting phenomena together: thermal, visual, spatial. Urban structure: Functional, mental, perceptual, visual. This principle can be used in the analysis as well as in the synthesis of urban design activities to explain complex systems involved. The system can be decomposed into its component levels or inter- acting levels. The complex systems are not comprehensive unless we simplify them by using alternative levels of description.

Hierarchical orders are seen in natural, social, technological, human and physical organizations such as physics, biology and society.

They are, however, especially applicable to the subject or objects which involve evolutionary process and developmental stages such as the hierarchy of goals, the hierarchy of systems and the hierarchy of values. In its application to architecture and complex systems, hierarchy simply means a set of Chinese Boxes. Opening any given box in a hierarchy discloses not just one new box within but a whole series of boxes. The best example of a hierarchical system can be seen in nature—a tree.

Integrative Rules and Principles of the Language of Urban Design 37

Central Place Theory is a well-known case of the application of the hierarchical concept to regional planning. The essence of this principle has been applied on a smaller scale to city design. The hierarchy of movement system in downtown Philadelphia and the concept of the essential/non-essential are two examples (Figures 18a and 18b).

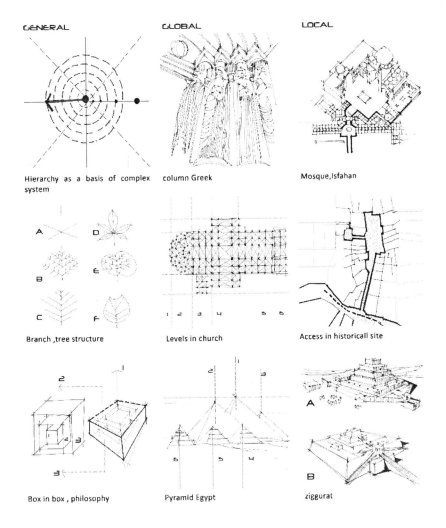

Figure 18a). The notion of hierarchy lies in the nature of very complex and evolving systems.

38 Hossein Bahrainy and Ameneh Bakhtiar

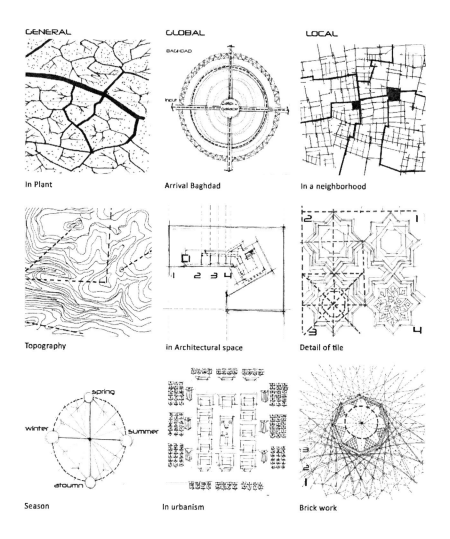

Figure 18b). Hierarchical order is the most natural way for ordering dynamic phenomena.

EQUILIBRIUM

This principle deals with all the dynamic and organic systems in the environment. The relationship of man to his environment is subject to continual and restless change from generation to generation, from year to year, and from instant to instant. This relationship is in danger of becoming disequilibrated.

There is a static equilibrium between Man and his environment or between inner and outer reality. The process of equilibrium is equilibration. Manipulative forms of equilibrium require the presence of two kinds of feedback, one negative (deviation-corrective) and the other positive (deviation-amplifying). Negative feedback tends to dominate the maintenance of equilibrium (socio-cultural, for example) at any given level. Positive feedback is required to move from one level to another.

Both negative and positive forms of equilibrium are always at work in the environment. Knowledge of the way in which they function in the decay and growth of metropolitan complexes is vital for urban designers.

The equilibration process governs the relation of man to his environment. Inorganic and Organic phenomena alike exist simultaneously in time and space and indeed within a fused Time—Space continuum. In progressively organizing and controlling his environment, Man has, therefore, involved himself with the continuous interplay of phenomena on the temporal and spatial dimensions. When human functions relate primarily to the spatial dimension, man conceptualizes models and fabricates tools essential to attain environmental control by using techniques for the organization of space.

Techniques to attain environmental control deal with the relationship of Man-to-Environment and Man-to-Man. Hence, these techniques are related to temporal as well as to biological factors. The social techniques comprise the tools or methods by which a community seeks to organize and retain environmental equilibrium. Examples of these are religious and philosophical concepts, legal codes, administrative systems, caste systems, ecclesiastical hierarchies, educational systems, economic institutions, etc. The principle of equilibrium implies that individuals, societies and their natural and built environment, as dynamic systems, are always in the process of change and self-correction. Self-correction is in the direction of equilibrium but equilibrium is not, of course, stable. The principle can also be applied to the evaluation of physical environment. The form of the city is subject to change and evolution. Some of the controls are deliberate and planned, but in general they go through incremental changes. When the conditions of disequilibrium are amplified, this might cause a shift to the next level of equilibrium. This, of course, would only be temporary. Urban design plays a significant role in the process of control and amplification.

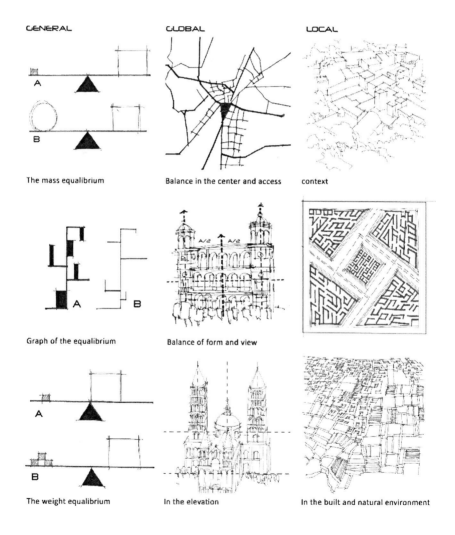

Figure 19a). Equilibrium deals with all the dynamic and organic systems in the environment.

Integrative Rules and Principles of the Language of Urban Design 41

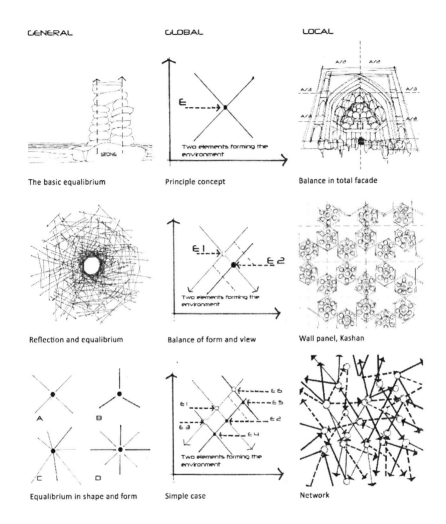

Figure 19b). The equilibration process governs the relation of man to his environment.

The changes that take place in the environment are orderly, i.e., they move and fluctuate within bounds. To go beyond the limits that are set (culturally, naturally, and ecologically) is to bring about destruction out of which, however, arise new bounds, restored equilibrium and a new order. Contrasting binaries of lack of fullness, openness, and closure create balance and counterbalance. These conditions are not static or mechanical. In the process of living in the environment, individuals and institutions adjust to the environment and tend toward a state of harmony and equilibrium (Figures 19a and 19b).

SIMILITUDE

Similarity is a relationship that holds between two perceptual or conceptual objects. Similarity between objects is not solely dependent on the characteristics of those objects. It is also affected by other present and immediately past stimuli, as well as long-term experience with related objects. The concept of *similar systems* is one of the most powerful concepts in the natural sciences, yet one of the most neglected concepts in philosophy of science today. It arose in physics, and appears to have originated with Newton in the seventeenth century. The concept was used in the nineteenth century in various fields of engineering (Froude, Bertrand, and Reech), theoretical physics (van der Waals, Onnes, Lorentz, Maxwell, and Boltzmann) and theoretical and experimental hydrodynamics (Stokes, Helmholtz, Reynolds, Prandtl, and Rayleigh) (Sterrett, 2016).

Similitude involves the juxtaposition of things not usually found together, or which have no ordered meaning together and the ambiguity that they create in terms of representation. Similitude sets up a heterotopic space (Foucault, 1983, 1986; Soja, 1990, 1996; Hetherington, 1996, 1997a) The Principle of Similitude in designing; it is a look at the physical pattern, which uses their basic units for shaping the complex final design. But the main structure of this principle Change through Time. The similitude in today's design means imitation and repetition of forms and creating unity through fixing the shape and importance of economic aspect without paying attention to its meanings, connections and social aspects. That is geometric similarity. The geometric approach to similarity does not go beyond the simplest representation of objects themselves, and in itself has little to say about the cognitive processes through which similarity relationships are determined (Shepard, 1987) As in "Foucault's Philosophy of Art" presents similitude as formal problems that shifting relation between subjectivity and truth. (Tanke, 2009) But in traditional design the

Integrative Rules and Principles of the Language of Urban Design 43

similarity, it is a kind of dynamic similarity, not merely a visual aspect. The "dynamically similar systems" that are similar in units and alphabet of design show different manner in different contexts. The outcomes of similarity in the past h5 4procedures based on the geometric idea can suggest the qualitative nature of the dimensions on which stimulus representations may vary and they can also suggest how that information is combined (Blough, 2001).

Figure 20. (Continued).

Figures 20a, b, c). Principle of dimensional homogeneity in historical site a. *Amir Chakhmaq* square b. Bazaar, *Yazd* c. dome of *Yazd* bazaar (photo by authors).

Figure 21. Principle of similitude in contemporary design.

In fact, the notion of similarity in the past was linked further, and more rigorously, into different kinds of connections, geometrical, meaning, cultural social and dynamical aspect. Space, by Varity, has tended to be associated with materials and their (often Euclidean) geometrical arrangements: the space between things, between physical entities that do not in themselves mean anything. Turning a space into a place, giving it meaning, it has been assumed, is the act of human intervention. There were many principles of geometry applied to designing of building such as form, space, shape, geometric proportion etc. Geometric ratio and proportions was very important tool used for aesthetic of building in ancient civilization. They have built structures with dimensions derived from mathematic constant and ratio such as golden mean, golden triangle, golden rectangle etc. This proportion system has lost its significance due to many more multiple design issues in modern context. The designers are more concerned about space utilization, energy issues, sustainable principle, form oriented buildings, structural design etc. These designers used to forget the essence of design lies in its aesthetic, without it buildings are just machines. There is need to understand the importance of geometric proportion in architectural design process (Gangwar, 2017) (See Figure 20 and 21).

GEOMETRY

IT is well known that formal design must be based upon exact geometrical construction. The history of art shows that the most beautiful places and formal design motifs are those depending upon definite and regular principles. The symmetry of design consists of the rhythmical repetition of certain parts of a design in relation to a plan or scheme as a whole, or uniformity as regards the answering of one part to another. The symmetrical forms of Nature have the same interdependence of detail. Even a casual examination showed that much of the harmony of relationship of parts in regular objects could be expressed graphically by geometrical lines. It was found by "experiment that this expression was very simple. In most cases, a few circles described concentrically would entirely satisfy zones of symmetry involved in some forms ("Natural Proportions in Architecture") (See Figures 22 and 23).

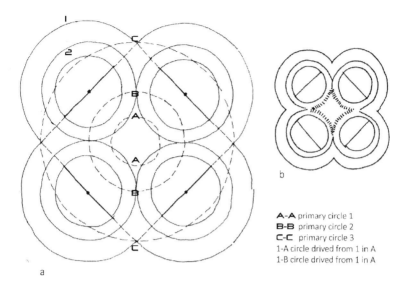

Figure 22a, b. a). The symmetry expressed formally and b): cross section of young fruit and contained seed of the verbena.

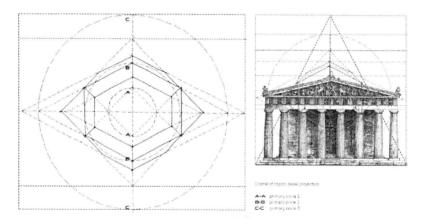

Figure 23. The crystal base contains the entire scheme of proportion and symmetry of found in the Parthenon.

As Albert Einstein says:" "Look deep into nature, and then you will understand everything better."– Albert Einstein. The relationship between geometry, nature and design is very important to understand because human beings are closely observing nature since their existence. The

Integrative Rules and Principles of the Language of Urban Design 47

human have started learning form nature and they have found that nature has geometric proportions in all her creation such as human, animals, and plants (Gangwar, 201) (see Figure 24).

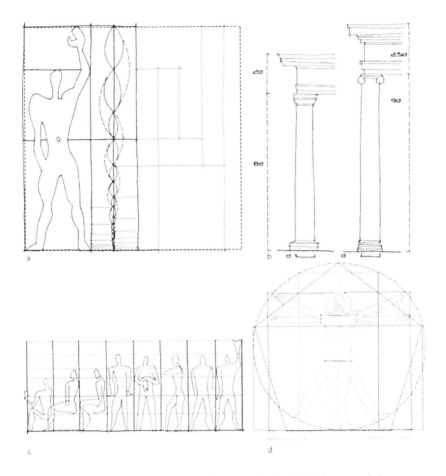

Figure 24 a, b, c, d. a). Le modular man by Le Corbusier b). Column modular geometry c). Anthropometrics through Le Modular Man d). Vitruvian Man

CYBERNETICS OR ENVIRONMENTAL FEEDBACK

Cybernetics or the science of feedback and control has tremendous potential for application in the urban design of the future. This is so because it is based on the ability to rapidly process an enormous amount of information and thus facilitate the making of appropriate decisions. It further conforms to the principle of self-correction. Such a device compares a current state of functioning with desired goals and adjusts performance on the basis of the observed differences.

Urban cybernetics, or the concept of environmental feedback, is indispensable in the complex environment of today. Each individual in this environment is in the midst of receiving, interpreting and sending huge numbers of signals and symbols as messages. The channels through which these communications flow are many and diverse, ranging from the very primitive devices of traditional cities to the most advanced electronic media of today. All of these sophisticated and complicated processes are sources and channels of actions and reactions, which result in the formation of the urban environment.

From the formal standpoint, urban cybernetics implies the transmission of visual and perceptual signals and reactions, which lead to decisions and actions which eventually change the physical environment. It also seems that this principle will be helpful in analyzing certain urban processes such as growth and locational decisions in which feedback plays an important role.

UNITY/MULTIPLICITY OR ORDER/DISORDER

Unity-multiplicity and order-disorder are binary sets which, in this form, are not contradictory but rather, complementary.

Unity is the fundamental principle of design and it is supported by all the other principles (Evans & Thomas, 2004, p. 5). Unity creates an integrated image in which all the elements are working together to support the design as a whole. A unified design is greater than the sum of its parts; the design is seen as a whole first, before the individual elements are noticed (Lauer & Pentak, 1995, p. 21). Unity implies order, rule, discipline, continuity, cohesion, certainty, and stability. While plurality means disorder, change, diversity, freedom, choice, flexibility, and discontinuity.

What is important is an optimum combination of these two principles to make a balance between the two. The dominance of any one over the other would lead to either chaos or imposed order, neither, which are desirable. What is desirable is bounded change, which means accepting change in limited boundary. Without one, the other is meaningless. The Greeks who used the word polis for city used the same word for a dice-and-board game that, rather like backgammon, depends upon interplay chance and rule (Joseph Rykwert, the Seduction of place).

Unity in societal actions and environmental forms means order and discipline; multiplicity, which is disorder, implies diversity, choice, freedom and openness. Unity stands for consistency and continuity and multiplicity stands for change, discontinuity and inconsistency. The essence of this principle is ordered change or change within certain bounds. These two entities, unity-multiplicity and order-disorder, may exist together in a complementary form of unity in multiplicity or order in disorder. Order and unity, in this sense, are dynamic and flexible, rather than static and fixed. Such an order achieves its form through fluctuation and multiplicity.

While order is a principle which controls and sustains all the parts of a system, disorder high- lights the existence of order through contrast. If there were no disorder, order would not be apparent. Order is a necessary condition for anything the human mind is to understand. Arrangements such as the layout of a city or building, a set of tools, the verbal exposition of facts or ideas, or a painting or piece of music are called orderly when an observer or listener can grasp their overall structure and the ramification of the structure in some detail. Order makes it possible to focus on what is alike and what is different, what belongs together and what is segregated. When nothing superfluous is included and nothing indispensable left out, one can understand the interrelation of the whole and its parts, as well as the hierarchic scale of importance and power by which some structural features are dominant, others subordinate (Arnheim, 2001). Order signifies a unity or purpose that transcends the parts or activities of a system. Unity transcends diversity and order pertains to the realm of unity and form. From the earliest times, order has been recognized as a principle apart from symmetry. Order has been regarded as beautiful and pleasant, disorder and excess as ugly and displeasing. From birth onward, Man struggles to establish a fragment of order in the infinite variety of his environment. The order attains results from the coalescence and transmission of diversified information. Common order is derived from the common symbol systems of a culture while multiplicity is left untouched.

Each of psychological, biological, physiological and physical systems of the human environment possesses a certain type of order. When the level of disorder in any of these systems exceeds a certain limit, it will lead to some kind of negative attitude toward the situation. This, in turn, will lead to the demand for change in the environment. A valid order should also be able to accommodate the circumstantial contradictions of a complex reality.

Order and unity belong to higher levels in the hierarchy of a society, whereas disorder and multiplicity are maintained at lower levels. Bacon has differentiated these levels into what is calls the "essential-nonessential." Essentials can be controlled to create order while non-essentials may be left to individuals to create multiplicity and diversity. The infrastructure, public facilities, and the like are examples of essential elements. Non-essentials are elements such as residential and related activities. This principle, therefore, is closely tied to the hierarchy principle.

This principle of unity-multiplicity and order-disorder will provide control and spontaneity, correctness and ease, complexity and contradiction in the urban environment. The domination of either one of these two elements over the other, either by exceeding or falling short of the imposed order will result in disequilibrium in the environment.

A good example of this is the case of standardization in cities brought about by legal (zoning ordinances) and economic (commercial forces) which have created a monotonous and homogeneous environment.

Concepts of this principle are invaluable in urban design. They combine realistic ideas for combining discipline and control with flexibility and freedom and thereby help to identify the scope of the authority and influence of urban design on public activity. The principle

Integrative Rules and Principles of the Language of Urban Design 51

can also help to define the extent and kind of intervention in urban design (Figures 25 and 26).

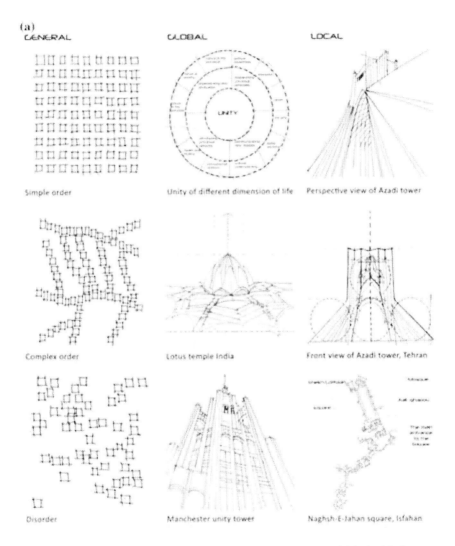

Figure 25. Unity-multiplicity and order-disorder are binary sets which, in this form, are not contradictory but rather, complementary.

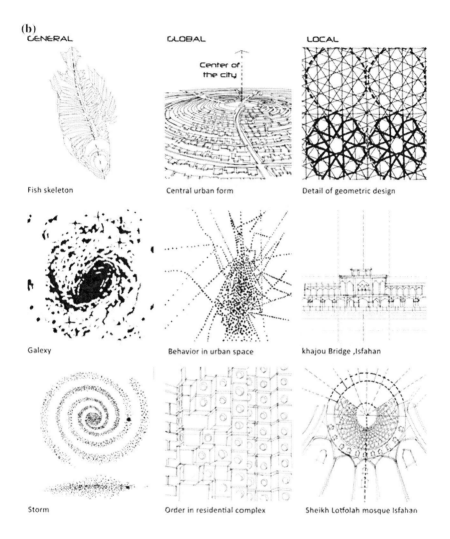

Figure 26. Unity implies order, while plurality means disorder.

MAN-ENVIRONMENT RELATIONSHIP

This relationship is characterized by the interaction between observers and observed. Man relates to his environment through his sensory experiences. To the elements of sensory experience belong the visual, aural and tactile elements. These experiences are transmitted to the mind by the nervous system through diverse receptor organs. These organs receive stimuli which are apprehended by the mind as the experienced sensations of color, shape, sound and texture.

SEMANTICS, METAPHOR AND ANALOGY

Semantics (semiology) is the theory of signs and their meanings. The fundamental idea of semiology and meaning in urban design is that any form in the environment or design in the language, is motivated or is capable of being motivated. Any form, even if it were initially arbitrary and non-motivated, becomes motivating because of its subsequent use. If a person is motivated by a form it means that the form conveys meaning and, therefore, fulfills a function. Urban semiology helps to ease the communication between man and his environment through signs, symbols, and their connotations. Interest in meaning and meaning making has proliferated in recent years. Meaning is considered crucial in understanding human experience and behavior. According to Morris (2011) signification and significance are a function of values. Values define the importance of a bearer of value in the human mind. Values are considered to have individual or collective criteria, which are the result of the individual's mind or the sum of the interaction of the one and the mind. It is the value of credit and privilege that human beings give to objectivity (Trieb, 1974). Places were essentially centers of meaning constructed out of lived-experience. By imbuing them with meaning, individuals, groups or societies change 'spaces' into 'places.' (Relph, 1976;as cited in Carmona, 2010, p. 97).

Meanings in the environment may be as varied and complex as people and human purposes. Meanings may include the knowledge latent in environmental forms and activities to which people are exposed; the knowledge gained as people learn the characteristics of their environment; and the knowledge upon which are based the plans of action used by people to satisfy their various individual and social purposes (Steinitz, 2007). By the sense (signification or semantics) of a settlement, is meant the clarity with which it can be perceived and identified, and the ease with which its elements can be linked with other events and places in a coherent mental representation of time and space and that representation can be connected with non-spatial concepts and values. Sense depends on spatial form and quality, but also on the culture, temperament, status, experience, and current purpose of the observer. Thus the sense of a particular place will vary for different observers, just as the ability of a particular person to perceive form varies for different places (Lynch, 1981, p. 131).

Smith in his syntax of cities book, in order to strengthen the position of human values in urban design, it tries to examine the range of rules governing the relationship between architectural elements and urban areas. Based on the syntax of cities, the components of the artistic environment give words that by way of putting them together creates a special meaning (Smith, 2013).

Hillier and Hanson emphasized the importance of the social meaning of the urban form. The living space of people is more than the sum of its material components. In this approach, space is considered as a body of subjective and social processes, and its function as and use is significantly related to its social application(Hillier & Hanson, 1989).

Schulz, with a phenomenological look at the environment, states that man is looking for its meaning through space presence which makes its existence meaningful and obtains a base in space and time(Norberg-Schulz, 1988). Meaning is not something apart from function, but is itself a most important aspect of function.

This importance of meaning can also be argued on the basis of the view that the human mind basically works by trying to impose meaning on the world through the use of cognitive taxonomies, categories, and schemata, and that built forms, like other aspects of material culture, are physical expressions of these schemata and domains. Physical elements not only make visible and stable cultural categories, they also have meaning; that is, they can be decoded if and when they match people's schemata (Rapoport, 1990).

Integrative Rules and Principles of the Language of Urban Design 55

Metaphors and analogies are similar. They both help to understand the world through interpreting certain regularities in imagination and creative thought. Metaphor is, fundamentally, a bringing together of images that have certain features in common and which are yet different, and more usually than not, drawn from different contexts, so that the juxtaposition of images per se and the significance of this juxtaposition stands out in clear relief. It is the imaginative representation of one thing in the form of another.

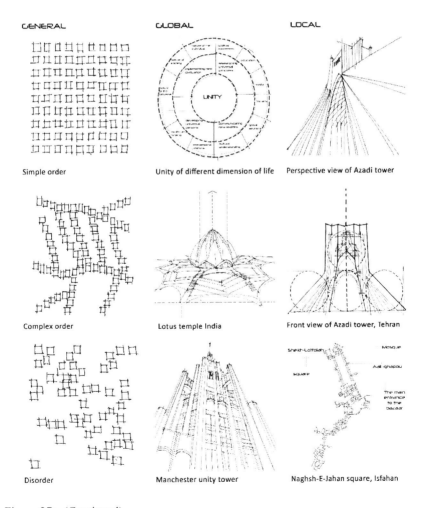

Figure 27a. (Continued).

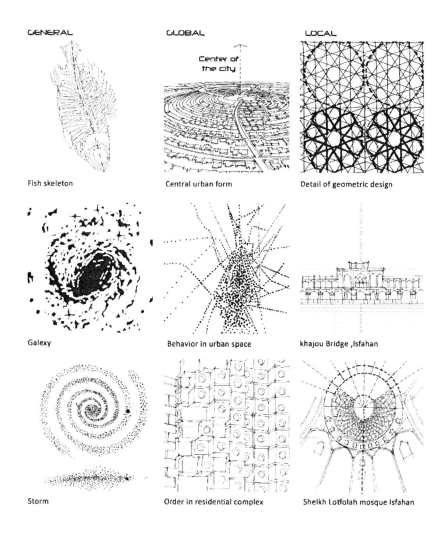

Figure 27a, b). The fundamental idea of semiology in urban design is that any form in the environment is motivated or is capable of being motivated.

While metaphor is a species of analogy, it is predominantly figurative. Analogy, like metaphor, is iconic, but its iconicity derives from more obvious or patent correspondences rather than on figurative extensions. Analogies between processes, events and objects can be useful tools for thinking in urban design. Using the real or seeming similarities of one thing and another, in attempting to describe what is less known from what

Integrative Rules and Principles of the Language of Urban Design 57

is already known, the description by analogy provides, in miniature, a picture of their association, of what is assumed to be the important aspect of the relationship of different things. The most convincing analogies are drawn from nature, because nature is a harmonious order in which many analogies are expressed between the different aspects of nature. In nature, the operation of all the parts comprises the harmony of the whole.

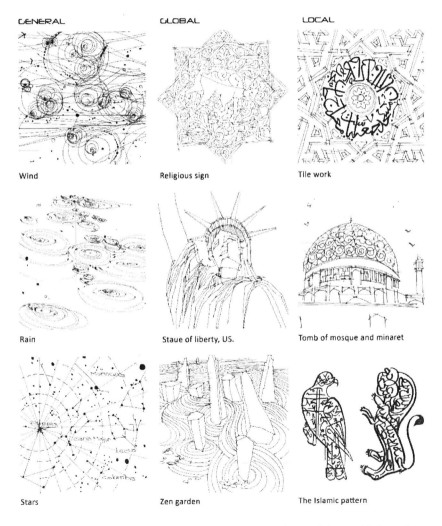

Figure 28. Semantics, metaphor and analogy help to understand the world through interpreting certain regularities in imagination and creative thought.

It is imperative that designers remain mindful of the dynamic interplay of various components of the meaning-making model and strive for more accurate and comprehensive measurement of meaning-making constructs. Through better measurement and study design, we can gain a better understanding of how people respond to and recover from form. Application of these elements is especially critical in that part of the design process where seeking the appropriate form to meet the established goals (which are normally of a socio-economic nature) is the major task of the urban designer. At this stage the urban designer attempts to translate words into form. Metaphors, semantics, and analogies, therefore, can be of great help in providing general ideas and concepts (Figures 27 and 28).

GENERAL SYSTEMS THEORY

The principle of the general systems theory is to facilitate the analysis and synthesis by way of reason and intellect. The idea of systems in urban design allows the analyst to study the context analytically as well as rationally. It helps him locate the problem and the appropriate solution to the problem. There are two valuable characteristics the significance of which is extremely helpful vis-a-vis our understanding of the environment and the problems that are associated with it. These characteristics are the idea of holism and the idea of rationality.

According to the idea or concept of holism, a system and the sub-systems and elements that constitute it are held together in such an integral manner that the entities thus held are bound together by an inseparable relationship. Rationality pertains to the principles by which these relationships and their characteristics are defined and accounted for. Rationality is regarded as being deterministic.

ORGANIZATION OF HUMAN ECOLOGY

This principle deals with the behavior of people in the social context. The relationship of man to man within the physical, social, economic and spiritual systems is the subject of this principle. It considers the systems that are important in the lives of people. People's spiritual spaces, interests and ambitions, values, needs and priorities, hopes, expectations, myths and responsibilities are some of the issues to be addressed by this principle.

Human ecology attempts to explain man's organized and collective relationship to his environment. It intends to explain social networks which depend on people's various means of physical mobility in getting to work, shopping, attending school, and their various degrees of economic mobility, depending on age, education, race, and income.

GESTALT

Gestalt phenomenon (or organized structures) are based on the claim that the meaning of the whole is greater than the sum of its components, or stated differently, that whole is greater than the sum of its parts. Gestalt theory argues against the validity of a systems approach because it holds that a system is not completely decomposable into its elements. Intuition, according to this principle, is the only approach that is capable of dealing with complex systems because it protects the meaning and integrity of the whole.

This principle has a significant application to urban design activities, especially with regard to the perceptual, visual and semantic aspects of the environment.

The Gestalt principle aids the understanding of problems by applying insight, which is a specific phase of productive thinking. It indicates that seeing into a problematic situation reveals its intrinsic structure.

Insight is the understanding that occurs when the situations reorganized in such a way as to become transparent—that is, when the essential features and the reciprocal relations are clearly and directly apprehended (Figure 29).

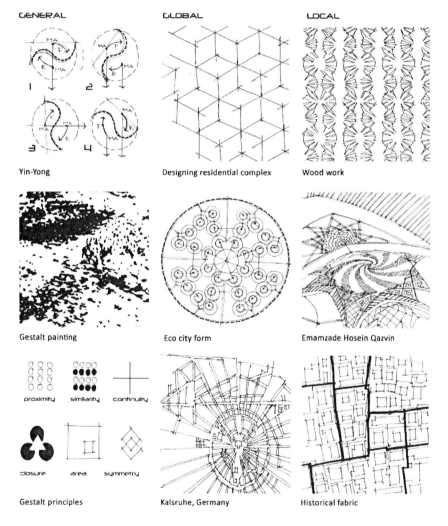

Figure 29. Gestalt principle is based on the claim that the meaning of the whole is greater than the sum of its components, or stated differently, that whole is greater than the sum of its parts.

CONTEXT AND CULTURE (LOCALIZATION)

A space is more properly conceived as abstract geometries (distance, direction, size, shape, volume) detached from material form and cultural interpretation (Gieryn, 2000).

The principles mentioned here as the rules and principles of urban design language, were intentionally thought of and formulated in such a way as to be abstract, general and universal. Their application in a specific environment, however, requires that great effort be made to modify them for that particular environment. In fact, there are very few of these principles that have universal applicability in the form in which they have presented here. Most of them, rather, are general principles which might be meaningless in certain environments unless they are modified and tested specifically for that specific culture or context. Each principle is described in an open and flexible way which can take on a variety of forms. It is the culture or context that makes them particularly meaningful (Ozgood and Tzeng 1990).

Lynch (1981, p. 101) states that physical patterns may have predictable effects in a single culture, with its stable structure of institutions and values. But it is not possible to construct a cross-cultural theory. It is even dangerous, since it will inevitably be used to impose the value of one culture on another. Each culture has its own norms for city form, and they are independent of those of any other.

Since the behavior patterns of different groups of individuals in different cultures vary, we may, therefore, conclude that their ways of life, their relationships with space and their interpretations of it also differ. This will imply the eventual need for specific rules and principles which are based on the value systems, aspirations, needs and problems of a particular culture. Depending on the culture in question, for example, the formal patterning of space and activities can take on varying degrees of importance and complexity. The organization of space, territory, boundaries, etc., is an important aspect of urban life which is closely tied to the attributes of the culture. It is for example, known that privacy can be defined only in a specific cultural context. What is regarded as a private place in a particular culture might be considered semi-private or even public place in another.

A similar cultural variability governs the interpretation and meaning of the space that contains the activities.

Culture is represented by certain shared values and interests. It comprises all aspects of a shared appreciative system, which is carved out by interests, structured by expectations and evaluated by standards of judgment. It is also a communication system of shared value. It is the shared values that modify these principles for the purpose of local application. Common symbol systems may be used as a clue to those values and interests.

A culturally specific urban design requires a culture-specific language of urban design based on culturally modified principles.

A characteristic of the present time is that worldviews must come to terms with the increasing exaggeration of both the global and the local. Urban designers should be in command of the following knowledge and skills (Bull et al. 2007, p. 228):

- The ecology and dynamics of natural and urban systems at a global, regional and local scale;
- The technologies of conservation, management and construction in the urban, suburban and natural domains (including 'sustainable technologies' as they evolve);
- The history and theory of practice, including the failures and successes of various projects in conserving, managing and constructing natural and urban areas;
- Spatial analysis of the processes of change That is manifested as urban areas and landscapes globally, regionally and locally; past and present;
- Conceptualizing the form and function of future, alternative territories et al. scales;
- Converting concepts into realizable urban projects, whether at the strategic or site scale;

Integrative Rules and Principles of the Language of Urban Design 63

- Communicating as cultural and cross-cultural practitioners across a wide range of territories; and
- The organization, legal framework and ethics of practice, globally and locally (Figure 30).

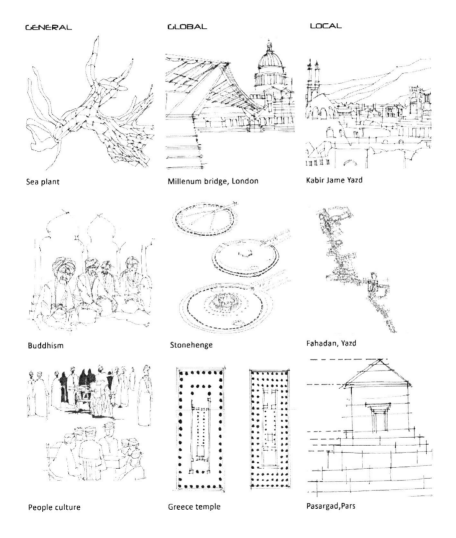

Figure 30. Application of principle in a specific environment requires that great effort to modify them for a particular environment.

SUSTAINABILITY

"The cities of the future, rather than being made out of glass and steel as envisioned by an earlier generation of urbanists, are instead largely constructed out of crude bricks, straw, recycled plastic, cement blocks and scrap wood. Instead of cities of light soaring toward heaven, much of the twenty-first-century urban world squats in squalor, surrounded by pollution, excrement and decay" (Davis, 2006).

Sustainable urban design is vital for this century, our health, welfare and future depends on it. We will need to develop flexible ways to 'shape' and design our future cities. Sustainable urban design is about balance in uses, density, transport, diversity, and natural and man-made environments. The urban world of the past century and a half is a phenomenon that has never existed before on this scale, and is coming into being at a staggering rate. It is becoming a new milieu, creating conditions of warfare, oppression, resistance, and tragedy that we only partially understand. A mega-scale view, such as that which archaeology can provide, is essential to understanding what is happening at the macro-scale of familiar public milieu and at the micro-scale of personal life. Humans have to learn, in their daily lives, how to cope with and exploit this new world and its frictions. We are still novices, trying out a myriad of strategies to try and learn what we should do and how to do it (Fletcher, 2010).

To some, sustainability implies self-sufficiency. There have been attempts to build self-sufficient villages often in remote rural areas. These are described by the Gaia Foundation as 'human scale, full featured settlements which integrate human activity harmlessly into the natural environment,' a worthy goal for any urban neighborhood (Eco-Village Foundation, 1994). These settlements grow their own food, generate their own power, and recycle their waste; coming as close as it is possible to an environmentally benign human settlement. But these are too small in scale and demand time and commitment from their members. In the case of cities, however, there are many who believe that cities are environmental disasters and have no place in a sustainable future that is until we consider

Integrative Rules and Principles of the Language of Urban Design 65

alternatives. More than half of the world's population now lives in cities so that it is hopelessly unrealistic to postulate a city-free sustainable future (Rudlin and Falk 2009).

Some principles are:

- Reducing input
- Using local resources
- Minimizing waste
- Making use of urban economies
- Walkability
- Personal safety
- Legibility
- Taming the car
- Creative congestion
- Higher density
- Public transport
- Reducing energy use
- Recycling
- Providing green space
- Mixed uses

Some of the urban design principles suggested for sustainable urban environment are (Thomas 2003):

- Sustainable urban structure, which deals with urban regions, the town or city and its rural and/or coastal hinterland
- The walkability
- Planning and design implications and opportunities
- Streets and street blocks, to enable direct pedestrian movement
- Optimizing development density
- Some density rules of thumb
- Some broader issues and key points, such as socially mixed and inclusive communities, provision of services and facilities that meet a range of needs, engaging local communities in discussion

about how they see their neighborhood and their priorities and aspirations for the future, provision of quality public transport services, the delivery of excellent local facilities and services, recognition that long-term management and maintenance are as important as the initial design and the vision of new development as catalyst for the improvement of existing areas (Thomas 2003, p 23).

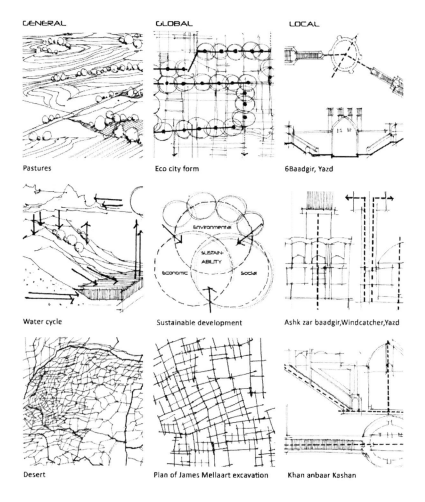

Figure 31. Sustainable urban design is vital for this century. Our health, welfare and future depend on it.

Bioregionalism has emerged as the new framework to study the complex relationships between human communities and the natural world. Bioregionalists believe that as members of distinct communities, human beings cannot avoid interacting with and being affected by their specific location, place and bioregion (Mc Ginnis M. V. 1999).

One of the principles outlined by Berg and Dasmann (1977) for bioregionalism is living-in- place, which means following the necessities and pleasures of life as they are uniquely presented by a particular site, and evolving ways to ensure long-term occupancy of that site. A society which practices living-in-place keeps a balance with its region of support through links between human lives, other living things, and the processes of the planet—seasons, weather, water cycles—as revealed by the place itself. One has to learn to live-in-place, in an area that has been disrupted and injured, by becoming aware of the particular ecological relationships that operate within and around it. A bioregion can be determined initially by use of climatology, physiology, animal and plant geography, natural history and other descriptive natural sciences (See also: Atkinson 1992 and Aberley 1994) (Figure 31).

ECONOMICS

Today the city is more than ever shaped by economic forces (Frey 1999, p. 1). Today's city is shaped by the communications and transport technology we use, and by market forces. In England, urban areas provide for 91 % of the total economic output and 89 % of all the jobs (Final Report of the Urban Task Force 1999). So valuation for sustainability cannot be separated from idea of actions whose effect is to sustain this or that form of life—in the cultural as well as ecological—economic sense (Abazaand Baranzini 2002, p. 33). It is for this reason that maintaining and improving the economic strengths of the towns and cities is therefore critical to the competitive performance of the country as a whole.

The planner's triangle, a model of sustainable development designed by Scott Campbell (1996), is based on three pillars: ecology, economy and equity. Knowledge of the structure and functioning of the urban economy is, therefore, fundamental to all urban design analysis and decisions. The density of an urban center is controlled by the extent and character of its productive and income-producing activity and its general vitality. Most metropolitan areas flourish because they serve as centers for production and distribution of goods and services, production and distribution functions create jobs, and employment opportunities attract people.

Crookston (1996) raising the question of: Urban design and urban economics: just good friends? From a review of a small group of settings, concludes that urban design thinking has made a real and integral contribution. Three things have to be done: Urban design needs to be better integrated into consultants' teams than it often is, sitting alongside urban economics as a discipline; and the successful projects show that it can. Urban design needs to be better integrated into the development control process than it often is. Urban economist need to be part of that integrated, collaborative approach too, working in a positive way to define the financially feasible and the economically sustainable, helping to overcome problems not just pointing out their existence.

- Land uses
- Activity locations
- Density
- Quality and quantity of infrastructure
- Job opportunities
- Taxation
- Financial resources
- Information and telecommunication technology

The marriage between telecommunications and computing along with the infrastructural networks for digital transformation of data, voice, image, and video—collectively known as information and telecommunications technologies (IT)—is increasingly gaining relevance

Integrative Rules and Principles of the Language of Urban Design 69

as a new dimension of cities. This dimension is partly physical and partly invisible and is forcing a reconceptualization of traditional urban models of city form and growth (Audirac 2002). These transformations posit a new kind of city that Hall (1997) describes as: globalized (connected to other cities in global networks); tertiarized and even quaternarized (dependent almost entirely for economic existence on advanced services); informationalized (using information as a raw material); and polycentric (dispersing residences, and decentralizing employment into multiple centers or edge cities. IT will affect the locational decisions of firms and households by dissolving the importance of distance and permitting foot loose economic activity to relocate to lower-cost exurban, rural and offshore areas. Telecommuting is working as a substitute for commuting trips. Workers substitute some or all of their working day at a remote location (almost always home) for time usually spent at the office (Wheeler et al. 2000). Firms will reduce office space costs, whereas telecommuters will have more freedom of choice in residential location. Depending on the density and frequency of office-trip substitution, telecommuting can con- tribute to the lowering of traffic congestion and ultimately to fewer carbon emissions.

Among the information and telecommunication tools the Internet has had the greatest, far reaching, and most permanent impact on the world economy and the transformation of society. As Castells puts it: our historic time is defined by the transformation of our geographic space.

Within cities, cyberspace contributes to a substantial reconstruction of urban space, creating a social environment in which 'being digital' is increasingly critical to knowledge, wealth, status, and power.

Castells (2000) has introduced a particular model of spatial organization, which, according to him, is characteristic of the Information Age, as the space of flows. He defines space of flows as the material arrangements that allow for simultaneity of social practices without territorial contiguity. It is made up of: (1) technological infrastructure of information systems, telecommunications, and transportation lines; (2) nodes and hubs; (3) habitats for the social actors who operate the network; (4) comprises electronic spaces such as websites, spaces of interaction, as well as spaces of one-directional communication. The growing use of telecommunications systems is doing far more than influence where people work and live, but is actually changing the character of activities that occur in the home, workplace, automobile, and the street. Telecommunications has made the fundamental elements of urban life—housing, transportation, work and leisure—far more complex logistically, spatially, and temporally (Moss, and Townsend 2000).

It seems, therefore, quite essential to consider IT and Telecommunications as an integral part of any urban design decision and take their implications on urban design elements into considerations.

GLOBALIZATION

The essence of globalization could be defined as the unrestricted movements of money, people, information, and culture. These agencies will have their effects on the components of urban form—urbanism, image and identity, spatial organization and structure, social ecology, public realm, scale and pace of development, and architectural vernacular. This process is especially significant in the case of the third world countries, where the conventional model of city becomes obsolete and cities are beginning to look more and more like that in the West (Pizarro et al. 2003).

Capital flows across the globe have markedly increased; a vast array of cultural products from different countries has become available in one place; and the nation-state is no longer the only entity that affects people's political life and ideas. Economy, culture, and polity are being transformed, reshaped and reworked to produce a more global world and a heightened global consciousness. Globalization takes place in cities and cities embody and reflect globalization. Global processes lead to changes in the city, and cities rework and situate globalization. Contemporary urban dynamics are the spatial expressions of globalization, while urban changes reshape and reform the processes of globalization (Short and Kim 1999). In addition, a loss of identity could be, as a result of a change and transformation of buildings and spaces, change of uses and function. The loss of association or desegregation or detachment also weakens place attachment. Researchers argue the incapability of the modernist approach in facing the contemporary issues including the deterioration of historical cities (Salama, 2009). When these happen, self or group identity will be disintegrated, as a result, of the losing of the identity. Sustaining the meanings and identity of the urban elements and icons (objects, structures and images) is important because they contribute to self-identity, sense of community and sense of place. Therefore, in any design effort, it is imperative to understand the level and form of attachment and meanings associated with the places to unravel place significance (Ujang, 2011).

PROCESS

Design is inherently a procedural entity, or a process. The concept of a process is widely present in various literature and design manuals, which attempt to produce a definition for design in general or urban design in particular. In fact, the concept of process is the core element of all these definitions. A process, which is normally considered as a continuous action, operation or series of changes that take place in a continuous manner, seems to be very relevant to any design activity. What is important is that design is a purposeful process that starts with some sort of objectives, and ends up with an outcome that responds to them.

Design process has always been a problematic and sensitive subject for designers. Many designers emphasize the art of design; that is, they seek expression of the intuitive and creative design capabilities of the individual designer. Others emphasize various systematic processes and take a philosophical approach to design (Shirvani, 1985).

There have been a number of efforts to model the process and procedures of urban designing (see for example: Barnett, 1966; 1982; Shirvani, 1985; Steinitz, 1979; Halprin, 1969; DeChiara and Koppelman, 1982; Bahrainy, 1998; Lang, 2005).

Most generic models suggest a rational step-by-step procedure that moves from perceptions of a problem to post-implementation evaluation of a completed work. While the models give some structure to our thinking and to our design of the decision-making appropriate to a job at hand, urban design does not take place in the neat sequential manner that the models suggest. Urban designing is an argumentative process in which participants in it learn as they go along. They learn about goals and means as perceived by different stakeholders, they learn from the evidence that each provides for its views. Application of process in urban design makes public involvement possible, prevents mistakes, makes generating alternatives and choice possible, makes issues understandable to the public and authorities, helps resolve conflicts and make consensus, facilitates implementation and effectuation, and finally, is inevitable for an activity as complex as urban design (Figure 32). During urban design, both the rational and the perceptual processes is the important stage. Since place is a space imbued with meanings, a design process of places should be approached and understood as a place represented by a total human experience: the physical elements and activities mixed with the socio-cultural and psychological components.

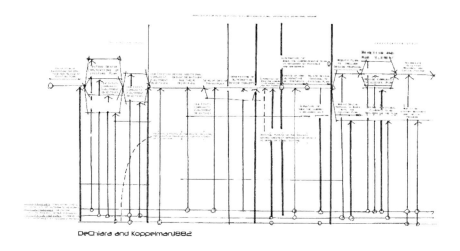

Figure 32. Designs is inherently a procedural entity, or a process (DeChiara and Koppelman, 1982).

Participatory and Collaborative

As there is a move toward equitable distribution of resources and opportunities, there is a move toward a broader consensus on the control and distribution processes. This ultimately leads to the 'user or citizen and can take the form of participatory planning and design (Smith 1973). There is a clear trend not just towards public consultation in design matters, but towards the public defining the principles of control and contributing to the administration of the control process itself. Such ventures provide a mechanism for managing disputes, and for giving the community far greater 'ownership' of the control mechanism (Punter 1999, p. 503). Community involvement in the process of urban design is increasingly promoted as a means of overcoming—or at least reducing—the professional/layperson, powerful/powerless and designer/user gaps. Participation takes many different forms, broadly conceptualized as top-down or bottom-up approaches (Carmona et al. 2003, p. 485, see also Bahrainy and Aminzadeh 2007, p. 241–270).

Participation makes dialogue, as 'the free flow of meaning between communicating parties, possible. There are some who emphasize the creative nature of dialogue as a process of revealing and then melting together the rigid constructions of implicit cultural knowledge. Forester (1989, 119–133) has addressed the issue of participation with the concept of 'designing as making sense together.' With the concept he refers to the notion of designing as a shared interpretive sense-making process between participants engaged in practical conversation in their institutional and historical settings.

According to Forester, such design work is both instrumentally productive and socially reproductive. Participants, however, may share a concern, but arrive at it through different cultural, societal and personal experiences. They belong to different 'systems' of knowing and valuing that will remain nearer or farther from each other in relation to the access to each other's languages. Design communication should therefore focus on reaching an achievable level of mutual understanding for the purposes at hand, while retaining awareness of that which is not understood (Healey 1992, p. 154).

The term collaborative design feature as an increasingly prominent part of the vocabulary as used in the range of planning and design literature. According to Healey (1997) collaborative planning and design is about why urban regions are important to social, economic and environ- mental policy and how political communities may organize to improve the quality of their places. Collaborative design is intended to serve as both a framework for understanding and as a framework for practical action.

Dobbins (2009) states that' the people who live where place improvement is happening must be involved; the disciplines whose work shows up in the process must coordinate; and the public-private partnerships that drive design and development in the public realm must work more aggressively to include the community voice. From the practical point of view, Brown et al. (2009, p. 111) explain how public involvement in the decision-making process was actually taking place in the case of AIA Urban Design winning projects. The process, they explain, began by identifying the kinds of participants to be included and laying out an approach intended to draw them into the process. Common mechanisms included community task forces, workshops, regular public meetings, charrettes, or some combination of all of them.

METHODS OF INQUIRY QUALITATIVE, ARTISTIC AND INTUITIVE METHODS

The last two principles have a two-fold function in the urban design language. One is the role they play a specific tools of analysis and synthesis. More important, however, is the role they play as the modes of thinking, the ideological framework of urban design process, decision and action. Intuition, as both a method of analysis and synthesis, plays a critical role in urban design. As a method of analysis and synthesis, it can be best applied to those areas of urban design, which are, by their nature, subjective, qualitative and subject to personal interpretation, modification and attitude. The perceptual, visual and aesthetic aspects of urban form and these processes which govern the relationship between man and environment are in the realm of intuitive analysis and judgment.

As a way of thinking, intuition plays a still more critical role in urban design. It attempts to integrate and unify all the various scientific and non-scientific methods into an integrated and unified language of urban design. Intuition in this regard, provides a holistic and gestalt perspective of the subject (urban form and urban activity systems), i.e., it considers all its parts and links simultaneously. It is thus a model of analysis and synthesis which stands against reductionism and, therefore, properly represents the reality and complexity of urban life. Intuition weaves the diversified methods and processes of urban design together as integrative tools and makes them more effective in their application.

METHODS OF INQUIRY QUANTITATIVE, SCIENTIFIC AND OBJECTIVE METHOD

According to Fecht (2012) urban designers traditionally have doubted the role that science can play in describing or predicting or fixing a city. They assert that cities have an emergent complexity that result from the interactions among people as well as between people and the environment, and that there is an element of human behavior that cannot be reduced to an equation. To survive Marshall (2012) argues that the field needs to incorporate scientific training into its educational curricula, and cultivate "a concern for testing and validation, critical assimilation of scientific findings from disparate sources, and dissemination of the most reliable, up-to-date findings." But as cities grow and researchers continue to elucidate the influence of design on factors such as carbon dioxide emissions, physical activity and quality of life, there will be an inevitable shift toward scientific thinking. The basic need for urban design to make use of 'urban science'

(Moudon 1992) or the 'science of cities' (Batty 2012) is for practical purposes uncontested.

The scientific method also plays a two-fold function in the process of urban design. As a way of thinking, the scientific method provides urban design language with rationality, perception and clarity. Given the complexity of the present urban environment as well as the nature of the democratic decision-making processes, the need for processes based on the scientific method is evident.

The scientific method, therefore, provides urban design with the reasoning aspect of thought. The interpretation of intuitive and reasoning modes can, however, create a more powerful, productive and creative context of thinking and ideology for urban design. The two, one with subjectivity, holism, originality and creativity and another with objectivity, rationality and universality can complement each other's deficiencies and shortcomings. This would imply the integration of emotion, feeling, and senses with the intellect, understanding and rational thought.

The second role of the scientific method in urban design is its effectiveness in providing effective tools and techniques for analysis, explanation, prediction, verification and evaluation of issues in urban design.

Applying these rules and principles, we may now define urban design as: The process of purposeful application of these integrative principles to the substantive elements of urban space and urban activity circuits to construct larger urban structures with the goal of creating formal and functional order in the urban environment.

Scientific thinking is regarded as logical thinking, as problem solving, as induction and as everyday thinking (Kuhn et al. 1988). But as Kahn (1969) says 'the measurable is only a servant of the unmeasurable, and ideally the two would be developed together.

INTEGRATIVE METHODS OF INQUIRY

It should be pointed out that according to Habermas it is a combination of three cognitive areas in which human interest generates knowledge that could lead to better understanding (analysis) and design (synthesis). They are: (1) work knowledge which refers to the way one controls and manipulates environment. This is commonly known as instrumental action—knowledge is based upon empirical investigation and governed by technical rules. The criterion of effective control of reality directs what is or is not appropriate action. The empirical-analytic sciences using hypothetical-deductive theories characterize this domain. Much of what we consider 'scientific' research domains—e.g., physics, chemistry and biology are classified by Habermas as belonging to the domain of work. (2) Practical knowledge: the practical domain identifies human social interaction or 'communicative action'. Social knowledge is governed by binding consensual norms, which define reciprocal expectations about behavior between individuals. Social norms can be related to empirical or analytical propositions, but their validity is grounded 'only in the intersubjectivity of the mutual understanding of intentions.' The criterion of clarification of conditions for communication and intersubjectivity (the understanding of meaning rather than causality) is used to determine what appropriate action is. Much of the historical-hermeneutic disciplines—descriptive social sciences, history, aesthetics, legal, ethnographic literary and so forth--are classified by Habermas as belonging to the domain of the practical. And (3) Emancipatory knowledge: the emancipator domain identifies 'self-knowledge' or self-reflection. This involves 'interest in the way one's history and biography has expressed itself in the way one sees oneself, one's roles and social expectations. Emancipation is from libidinal, institutional or environmental forces which limit our options and rational control over our lives but have been taken for granted as beyond human control. Insights gained through critical self-awareness are emancipator in the sense that at least one can recognize the correct reasons for his or her problems. 'Knowledge is gained by self-emancipation through reflection leading to a transformed consciousness or 'perspective transformation.' Examples of critical sciences include feminist theory, psychoanalysis and the critique of ideology, according to Habermas.

Summary of Habermas' three domains of knowledge Habermas' three domains of knowledge their related methods have very strong and meaningful implication for the practice of urban design. In fact the very nature of the field of urban design makes the integrative application of these methods inevitable.

Summary of Habermas' three domains of knowledge

Type of human interest	Kind of knowledge	Research methods
Technical (prediction)	Instrumental (causal explanation	Positivistic sciences (empirical-analytical methods)
Practical (interpretation and understanding	Practical (understanding)	Interpretive research (hermeneutic methods)
Emancipatory (criticism and liberation)	Emancipation (reflection)	Critical social sciences (critical theory methods)

(See: Roderick 1986; Schroyer 1973; Healey 1996; Forester1993).

Chapter 4

THEORY-PRACTICE RELATION IN URBAN DESIGN

To Alexander (2015), there is no planning—only planning practices, and Raelin (2007) states that theory loses much of its vitality if uninformed by reflection on practice.

Urban design and planning practice have attracted the attention of numerous scholars and critics during last several decades. For example: Watson (2002); Alexander (2012); Alexander (2010); Alexander (2015); Saarikoski (2002); Duning (2004); March (2010); Kerry R. Brooks, Barry C. Nocks, J. Terrence Farris, & M. Grant Cunningham (2002); Healy (2011); Boelens (2011); Dyckman (1969); Abukhater (2009); Lisa A. Schweitzer, Eric J. Howard, & Ian Doran (2008); Forester (2012); Boelens (2010); Binder (2012); Watson (2012); Raelin (2007); Dandekar (2018); Davoudi (2015); Lisa A. Schweitzer, Eric J. Howard and Ian Doran (2008); Kelvin MacDonald, Bishwapriya Sanyal, Mitchell Silver, Mee Kam Ng, Peter Head, Katie Williams, Vanessa Watson & Heather Campbell (2014); and Rosenbloom (2018).

In the case of urban design practice, however, there have not been as many research as in urban planning, see for example: Bahrainy and Aminzadeh (2007, Bahrainy and Bakhtiar (2016), Elshater (2014), Moudon (1992, 2003), Grade 2008, Orly Linovski and Anastasia

Loukaitou-Sideris (2012), Hyungun Sung, Sugie Lee, and SangHyun Cheon (2015), Inam (2011), Southworth, M. 1989, Punter, J. 2007, Lang, J. 2006, and Brown, J. L., D. Dixon, and O. Gillham, 2009.

John Friedmann (1987, 38-44) regards the definition of planning as the link between knowledge and action. But planning theory has been of little use to planning practitioners (see Campbell and Marshall, 1998; Sanyal, 2002).

Inam (2011) claims that a conventional assumption about theory and practice is that they represent a dichotomy of types of thinking and knowledge; that is, a division into two mutually exclusive or even contradictory groups. Theory represents a type of thinking that is a generalized abstraction of observations for the purpose of explaining other observations, and theoretical knowledge is judged by how well it explains and even predicts as wide a range of phenomena as possible. Practice, in contrast, is conventionally dependent on a more instrumental conception of knowledge in order to help us accomplish things and proves its worth by how well it helps to accomplish whatever needs to get done. This type of dichotomy suggests that theory is general and abstract, while practice is specific to a set of tasks. The dichotomy has played a considerable role in the progression of complex design theory, while keeping practice relatively straightforward without overly complicated demands on its task-oriented knowledge base. The dichotomy is reflected to an extent in the growing significance of research and publications in academia on the one hand, and the growing trends of so-called best practices at the cutting edge of professional work on the other. There are few theories in urban design that fit the breadth and depth of the definition presented before.

All these show that there have been different interpretations of the term "theory" in general and in urban design specifically, and therefore, there exist some piecemeal and sporadic statements developed by different people for their specific needs and interests.

One reason for this so-called theory/practice divide is that there has been a proliferation of theories proposed to understand planning processes and outcomes (Allmendinger, 2002a, 2002b). The crux of this 'disconnect' between theory and what practitioners do is the failure of academics to develop theories that provide a useful analysis of the planning system which can inform change (e.g., change that leads to more democratic processes or environmentally sustainable outcomes) and are of real use to practitioners (Hillier, 2002).

There has been an emergence of a distinct and identifiable approach to the theorizing of planning. Broadly termed the *practice movement* (Liggett 1996), this new approach is characterized by the study of individual planners and planning practice: the documentation and analysis of the many and varied activities of planners, their products, their interactions, and their impacts. The assumption is that it is possible to learn from practice to inform practice. This raises some central questions: Can documented accounts of experience contribute to learning? What theoretical and methodological approaches to the understanding of practice can best fulfill its pedagogical potential? And what form can "practice writing" most usefully take? Different forms of practice writing are evident in recent literature, and this offers an opportunity to assess the usefulness of this kind of work.

But proponents of the practice movement claim that their highly specific, context-bound accounts of planning activity are able to bridge the gap between theory and practice and are able to give better insight into the nature and possibilities of planning practice than previous theories were able to do (Innes 1995). Sources of theory that could be drawn on to develop this model: phenomenology, language philosophy (Wittgenstein), linguistics, ethno methodology, pragmatism, and ideas put forward by Habermas—critical theory. John Forester, later to become a leading contributor to the practice movement, was a student of Krieger's when he introduced Habermasian ideas to his planning students in the early 1970s (Martin Krieger, personal communication, 14 September 1997). Howell Baum (1983, 1986, and 1996) was another central figure in the development of this approach.

Ultimately, a practice epistemology should be able to target learning outcomes that are specifically practice based, in other words, that derive from learning within the practice world rather than from the classroom (Raelin, 2006).

Within the practice movement, the communicative planning theorists appear currently to hold a dominant position, largely inspired by the writings of Habermas. Although writers within this position (Forester, Healey, Hillier, Hoch, Innes, Mandelbaum, Throgmorton, and others) often follow significantly different lines of argument, this approach focuses broadly on processes of communication and knowledge production in planning.

The same assumption about theory and practice in urban planning is also true in urban design, so that they represent a dichotomy in which theory represents abstract thinking to explain observations, while practice depends on a more instrumental conception of knowledge to help accomplish tasks. The theory/practice relationship in urban design can take a number of mutually beneficial forms, especially dialectical ones. Also since urban design is a complex and multifaceted field, the most useful theories are ones that are integrative (i.e., that incorporate function, form and process) rather than singular (e.g., based almost exclusively on ideas of green design, technology or historicism). (See for example the experimental urban design studio for graduate students at the Massachusetts Institute of Technology in 2009, Kevin Lynch's book Good City Form).

In professional practice, there is a welcome trend to broaden both an understanding of urban design as a field and to be more inclusive of its practice, for example, by incorporating the work of landscape architects (e.g., ecological systems approaches) and planners (e.g., public policy and land use regulation). For example, an emerging theme in the field is that of landscape urbanism, with its promise of integrating land use, ecological systems thinking and distinctive place making (Waldheim, 2006).

Thus, while contemporary discussions on urban design show some promise, these discussions still continue to focus almost exclusively on matters of form, including new ways of organizing cities (e.g., Krieger & Saunders, 2009), or new types of neighborhoods, commercial corridors, edge cities and downtowns (e.g., Barnett, 2003), rather than the fundamental processes by which we choose priorities, address challenges and conceive of the future city. Such processes are particularly relevant to the complexity inherent in contemporary cities: the world is becoming increasing urban with the majority of the population now living in cities; cities are the primary sites of crises such as lack of economic opportunities or adequate shelter, and the fastest growing and most complex urban areas are now in the developing regions of Asia, Africa and Latin America (UN Habitat, 2009). These challenges are as much about process as they are about form; and urban designers can bring to bear their knowledge, experience and creative talents on rapidly changing cities, provided they have the appropriate conceptual tools.

In order to be truly relevant to the critical challenges that cities face (e.g., infrastructure deficiencies, affordable housing, transportation choices, efficient use of scarce resources) and to the policy making and private decisions that shape cities (e.g., land use regulations, tax incentives, profit motives), urban designers must better understand and more directly affect the processes that shape cities. Moreover, a close reading of histories of urban form reveals that physical structures, spaces and systems are the ongoing result of multiple processes (e.g., Kostas, 1991; Loukaitou-Sideris & Banerjee, 1998; Marshall, 2004). Two crucial aspects of city-building processes are ways of conceptualizing the integration of multiple issues into the design process, and the reflections on actual practices of urban design as sources of emergent theory.

The experimental urban design studio conducted in Boston, USA at the Massachusetts Institute of Technology (MIT) in 2000 as an interrogation/reinterpretation of theory of Good City Form as a source of an integrative, rather than a singular, approach to contemporary urban design.

There are few theories in urban design that fit the breadth and depth of this definition, and Good City Form is one of those rare ones. The primary asset of the theory of Good City Form is that it embodies an integrative approach grounded in the reality of practice. The professional practice of urban design involves multiple and often conflicting stakeholders and objectives. Such situations require the challenging tasks of establishing priorities and making difficult trade-offs rather than the singular and overly-narrow approaches suggested by green design, landscape and neotraditionalism. This is because urban design needs to simultaneously address a wide range of issues such as economic development, social justice, choice of housing types, access to a variety of transportation modes and adaptive reuse of historic urban fabrics.

Lynch's accessible and indeed democratic concepts of urban design are in marked contrast to theorists who conceptualize the field in extremely narrow terms, such as an extension of the architectural imagination or the physical consequences of government politics (Cuthbert, 2006, p. 9).

There is little contemporary research on the relationship between design theory and professional practice. Theories of urban design offer a set of general directions that can be translated into specific design strategies depending on the context, while at the same time establishing criteria to evaluate existing places without demanding that all cities reach these criteria in the same way. The challenge for design theory is to not be, on the one hand, so abstract as to be far too difficult to translate into practice (as some practitioners have found with the work of urban theorist Ed Soja), while on the other, to not be overly narrow and prescriptive (as critics claim to be the case with New Urbanism).

Many contemporary design theories achieve clarity by focusing on only one or two aspects of city building. For example, parametric urbanism claims to be a new style of urban form using the cutting edge techniques of computer simulation and form-finding tools, as well as parametric modeling and scripting (Schumacher, 2009, p. 15). Another example is landscape urbanism, which describes disciplinary realignment in which landscape replaces architecture as the basic building block of cities (Waldheim, 2006, p. 11). While the former chooses almost exclusively to focus on the relationship between technology and form, the latter devotes most of its attention to natural elements such as topography, vegetation and water. While both these theories introduce crucial elements into conceptual discourses on the contemporary city, they also neglect other important facets, such as ways of enabling less privileged residents to reach vital resources (e.g., Lynch's dimension of 'access') and enabling residents to have a greater say in the future of their city (e.g., Lynch's dimension of 'control'). In contrast, Lynch attempts to integrate the complex and multifaceted nature of city-building, albeit at the cost of greater focus and clarity.

The experimental studio (Inam, 201, 259) demonstrated ways in which the theory/practice dialectic creates a highly reflective and adaptable framework for urban design practice, as opposed to the narrowly defined formula with its claims to the 'right approach', often seen in approaches based primarily on historicism, technology or green design.

Instead of an ontological definition for urban design, some have found it easier to examine urban design's practical applications (Orly Linovski1 and Anastasia Loukaitou-Sideris, 2012). Indeed, as Southworth (1989, 369) argues, urban design plans record the values, intentions, and methods of urban designers in shaping a city's physical environment.

Practice is said to be the "institution of meaning", that is knowledge-centered practice. The knowledge-centered practice is "a set of doings and sayings organized by a pool of understandings, a set of rules … and common and collective ends, projects, emotions and beliefs" (p. 53). These practices are "socially recognized forms of activity, done on the basis of what members learn … capable of being done well or badly, correctly or incorrectly" (Barnes, 2001: 19) and endowing their "membership with the power to perform" (p. 20).

This is an "epistemic practice" (Knorr-Cetina, 2001: 175). Here, practice means more than simple skill or routine task-performance, but involves specialized knowledge and expertise. Epistemic practices can operate in various fields, each with its distinct epistemic culture. These fields are not limited to the exact sciences, but relate to their specific "epistemic objects," which may be real-objective natural things or cognitive-cultural artifacts—in Knorr-Cetina's term, "scientifically-generated objects" (pp. 175–178). It follows that understanding and identifying a particular epistemic practice involve learning and defining its relevant "expert–object relationship" (Knorr-Cetina, 2001: 187). However, it seems that contemporary plans display fewer types of methods, less analytical rigor, and less emphasis on participatory practices than previous generations of plans (Orly Linovski1 and Anastasia Loukaitou-Sideris, 2012).

Learning from Practice

The notion of learning from practice to assist practice is therefore a central one. Experience can yield a more useful learning process than, for example, learning from general theories or rules. Past experience constructs an understanding appropriate to the new situation. It is necessary to begin to understand how the rules can be applied under different conditions or in differing contexts. Expertise is achieved only on the basis of a great deal of experience of real-life and varying situations. Ultimately, the response of the expert becomes intuitive rather than based on a consideration of which rules to apply.

There is, therefore, support for the idea that the ability to perform (a professional task) depends on the practitioner's ability to bring past accumulated experience fruitfully to bear on the problem in hand. For the practice movement, however, two important questions remain. Practitioner learning, be fostered by indirect experience in the form of texts and reports of practice experiences, that is, through "mediated learning," as well as by direct encounters with reality? Can academics or planning theorists thus play a role in improving practice by documenting, analyzing, and reflecting on the experience of practitioners?

Case studies of planning, which lend themselves at least to partial demarcation potentially offer a framework for interrelating actors, circumstances, contextual settings, and sequences of events. The case study, Fischler (1998) suggests, is the primary weapon of the planning theorist. Research methodologist Yin (1994) argues that case studies are the preferred research method "when 'how' or 'why' questions are being posed . . . and when the focus is on a contemporary phenomenon within some real-life context" (p. 1).

Fischler (1998, 2000) has suggested history is a source of good case studies of planners in action as it provides instructive precedent and it is of great value in explanatory planning theory when we want to understand why planners act in particular ways, as well as understand what they do.

Accounts of planning practices that are rich in contextual detail also allow readers to add to their mental repertoire of unique instances of planning and to judge the extent to which there are sufficient points of similarity with a current problem for it to be useful. Perhaps one of the most difficult problems that have to be faced when trying to draw on understandings or ideas developed in a different context is that of how transferable they are: What is unique to a particular time and place, and what is more general?

Hoch (1996, 43) has suggested that planners become "storytellers of practice." The building of a mental repertoire of many such narratives and cases can provide the basis for the kind of expert judgment required in the day-to-day work of planners.

Documented planning practices provide a vehicle for learning and have found support for this from the disciplines of education and experiential learning. One of the significant values of in-depth case-study research that takes the form of fully contextualized stories of planning and design practices (Watson, 2002) is documentation and analysis.

There is no doubt that planning and design theories affect practice (Alexander, 2010) to the extent that some (Alexander, 2015) claim that "there is no planning—only planning practices." The same argument might true in the case of urban design. By documenting and analyzing experiences and learning how practice is actually shaping, it becomes possible to theorize planning and then use that knowledge (theory) in similar situations (March, 2010; Binder, 2012).

Chapter 5

PRACTICAL APPLICATION OF THE URBAN DESIGN RULES AND PRINCIPLES: LESSONS LEARNED FROM THE PAST

At its inception, the Iranian city was a reflection of cosmic order. This could be seen in the ancient Iranian cities. In fact, in the past, cities and spaces were bearing messages from other worlds which were shaped according to cosmic, philosophical and sacred orders. So a variety of shapes and forms were used on the basis of multiple design principles to express higher order facts. Here in this section, effort is made to explore the integrative design principles in the various orders and layers of selected examples of Iranian urban spaces. This is to reflect some signs of this order and coordination, which, on one hand, represent design principles and, on the other hand, represent cosmic order as principal and intrinsic aspects in design.

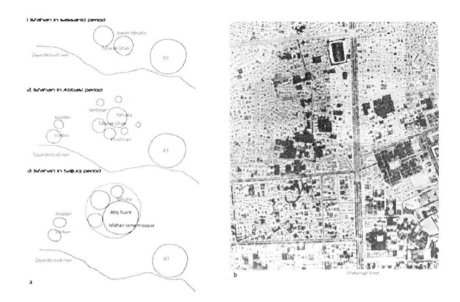

Figure 33a, b). Formation and evolution process of the main structure concept and its role in the design of the city of Isfahan: a (1: *Sassanid* period, 2: Abbasid period 3: *Saljuqi* period) b: *Chaharbagh* street (Iran cartographic center, Isfahan 1956).

ISFAHAN AND ITS GENERAL STRUCTURE

The main patterns of the general structure of city of Isfahan are mountains, river, streets, regular and geometric lots, both square and rectangle, which are shaped by using strong geometry with a unified pattern and proportions, but generally complex configuration (Figures 33 a and b and Figure 34)

Gradually this tempo-spatial order is used not only in the general configuration of the city but also in the design of various forms and spaces, even in micro spaces and details (Figure 35).

One of the examples to show how this order created and developed in coordination with design principles in a balanced manner is *Naghse Jahan* square in Isfahan. A careful analysis of the application of principles in this space reveals that, although each of these principles may be recognized separately, the primary quality of the space is the interaction and balance

Practical Application of the Urban Design Rules and Principles 91

of these different principles of design which lead to the creation of an overall order and balance. These principles may be clearly seen in the square façades and also in the elements and main features. Their combinations in space create beauty, so that in spite of the passing of time, the square continues to keep its dynamic and sustainable character, which reflects the valuable and rich architecture. This is the same substance and meaning that is derived from rational order, which is reflected in the existence order and have based their design principles toward this eternity. So these principles are of abstract nature, which intend to portray symbolic meaning, substance and order in the tangible space and form and thereby direct the addressee to receive cosmic order, which will create and develop beauty.

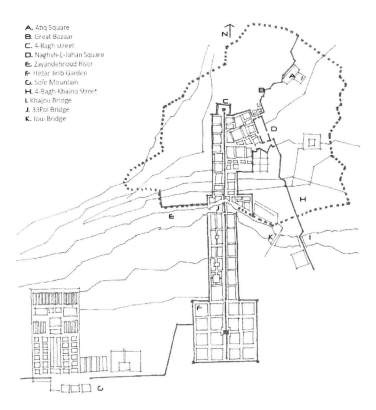

Figure 34. Order in the main structure of the city was based on organizing natural and built environments.

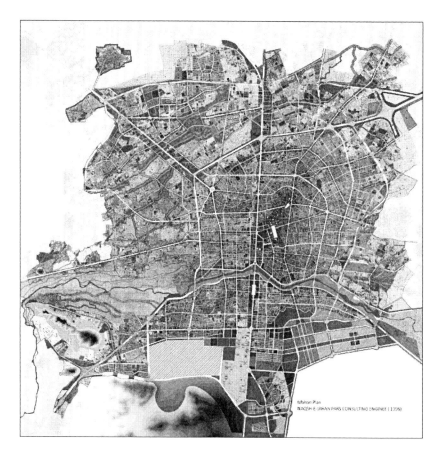

Figure 35. Map of contemporary Isfahan (1996).

According to Plato, "since philosopher deals with the world of ordered ideas, he will become ordered himself to the extent possible for human nature, and then enters into ideas that had seen in that world in the life of individuals and communities" (Plato, 1943).

In fact, Man has always believed in the analogy between him and his world, and the cosmic world. This principle has been valid as a basis for design from ancient Iran through later eras. It invites the addressee to focus on the tangible order and recognize the original order. Of course identity, culture and people's motivation to be present in space are also effective in this perception. However, in spite of differences in certain spaces, it seems that the designer has more successful relations with common human

Practical Application of the Urban Design Rules and Principles 93

characteristics and visions. As Marshall states: "urban order is not solely related to humans with their individual interests, but it deals with a group of people." (Marshall, 2009) He further believes that these principles and orders talk to addressees through analogical language.

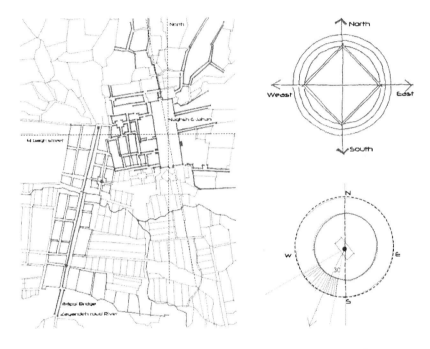

Figure 36. The principal orientation of form and space were based on optimum orientation with regard to climatic considerations.

Therefore, although the knowledge base of urban design and its principles are considered as an ordering factor in various physical, structural and spatial scales and signify the spatial-structural organization, these principles, aside from the functional, aesthetics, and applied roles, also affect the receiver's perception of the content and eventually create a reaction in his/her behavior. Aside from the visual form, the design principles play a dynamic role in the type of reaction and behavior in space. The principles are based on creating quality in place. In this design thinking, the patterns and the fundamental design units are shaped in a general system and, with a symbolic role and artistic expression, express metaphysical concepts in a way that are comprehensible to the receiver. So, the principles, aside from creating physical order, seek to consciously guide the audience in the system of existence. Therefore, space is not just determined by orderly and pure lines and geometrical and mathematical forms, but is weighted and valued through design principles and this numinous system, which has qualitative and symbolic aspects.

In order to explore the application of the design principles in the *Naghshe Jahan* square, expert groups were first asked to identify from the 20 principles mentioned in the previous chapter the ones that are most dominant in the design of the square. The selected principles were then separately studied at three levels: urban space, architectural space and design details in the square. Architectural spaces were selected by visitors in the square, details which will be given later.

A questionnaire was designed to more thoroughly investigate the application of the design principles in the *Naghshe Jahan* square. One hundred individuals from professors and PhD students in architecture and urban planning were asked to select the most effective principles, from the principles discussed in the previous chapter, used in the perpetuity design of the space. The results, are shown in Table 1, where the numbers in the first column indicate number of people mentioned certain principle. In Table 2 the results of the photography angles, selected by visitors, are shown.

Here in this part, which is intended to verify and confirm the actual role of the proposed principles in the design of spaces, real application of those principles will be recognized in a selected urban space. Theoretical discussions in previous chapters led to a series of design principles, which their practical application had to be tested in a real world situation.

The main approach for information gathering is through indirect observation, by which verifiable evidences are reached to support theoretical basis. For this purpose, *Naghshe Jahan* Square, in the historical section of the city of Isfahan, was selected as case study. The basis for data gathering, interpretation and analysis was visitors' perceptions of the environment. This is an indirect approach, so that considering the purpose of the study and the significant role of the general public and common

Practical Application of the Urban Design Rules and Principles 95

collective view in the perception of design principles, the visitor is pulled into the research scene. The researchers, then, scrutinize their findings with the data gathered by the visitors (Figure 37).

Figure 37. Some viewers while taking photos.

The visitors were asked to take only one single photo from the most beautiful element of the square, and then explain why they chose that element. Repetition of certain angles and elements in the photos lead us to the study and analysis of design principles on the basis of visitors' preferences. In this approach visitors are considered the actual actors, not passive viewers, in public spaces. So that visitors select desired dimensions in relation to tangible realities through their mental processes. Then by classifying and analyzing these dimensions on the basis of theoretical framework presented in previous chapters, final conclusions on the validity of principles will be made. This method is designed in a way that people (visitors) may reflect their perceptions of the environment, but the task of perceptions interpretation will be done by experts.

In fact, in this approach, visitor is mainly responsible for his/her action at the beginning of the study and feels quite free in selection and choice of the subject. Personal knowledge, self-determination and responsibility are determinant factors for visitor's choice. When pictures are taken, visitors are asked to explain why that angle/element was chosen and to present reasons why they consider the chosen subject attractive to them.

Table 1. Valuation of design principles

N	Principles
52	Symmetry
93	Patternization
65	Quantization
84	Centrality
50	Boundries
8	Territories
72	Binary
57	Hierarchy
91	Equilibrium
46	Cybernetics
96	Unity-Multiplicity
73	Order-Disorder
90	Semantics-Metaphor
14	Gestalt
88	Context-Culture
69	Dynamics
58	Continuity
42	Sustainability
67	Diversification
70	Geometry

Practical Application of the Urban Design Rules and Principles 97

Table 2. Photography angles

P	N	Angle of Photography	
19.3	63	SHEIKH LOTFOLAH MOSQUE	One Space
0.9	3	GHEISARIEH BAZAAR	
42	137	SHAH ABBAS MOSQUE	
7.4	24	ALI QAPU PALACE	
0.9	3	SHEIKH LOTFOLAH MOSQUE & GHEISARIEH BAZAAR	Two or more spaces
8	26	SHEIKH LOTFOLAH MOSQUE & SHAH ABBAS MOSQUE	
17.8	58	SHAH ABBAS MOSQUE & ALI QAPU PALACE	
0.3	1	ALI QAPU PALACE	
1.8	6	SHAH ABBAS MOSQUE & ALI QAPU PALACE & SHEIKH LOTFOLAH MOSQUE	
100	326	SUM	

f	fi	Angle of Photography
23	98	SHEIKH LOTFOLAH MOSQUE
2.8	12	GHEISARIEH BAZAAR
53.3	227	SHAH ABBAS MOSQUE
20.9	89	ALI QAPU PALACE

What follows is the validation and confirmation of the proposed principles by using observation method (space photography) and through objective and perceived analysis of one of the successful experiences of urban design.

As the photos show, the photography angle repeated most was *Shah Mosque*, which includes design principles in a prominent and comprehensive way, in different design dimensions of form, space and activities. Principles are reflected in all documents (plan, façade, sections and internal and external human views). Majority of national visitors mentioned the reason for selecting this angle as: aesthetics, semantics, symbols and meaning dimensions. While for foreign visitors, aesthetics, geometry, centrality and details were determinant factors (Figure 38).

Figure 38. Some of the photos taken by viewers at the square.

Here a perceptual and objective analysis will be performed on one of the successful examples of architecture, that which is the most dominant element of the square and was selected by viewers.

Pattern Principle

As it was mentioned in chapter 4, repetition and order are the two essential factors in the patternization process that lead to the creation of the ratios and relations between design factors and lead to the foundational units of the design patterns which create structure for the space (Figure 39).

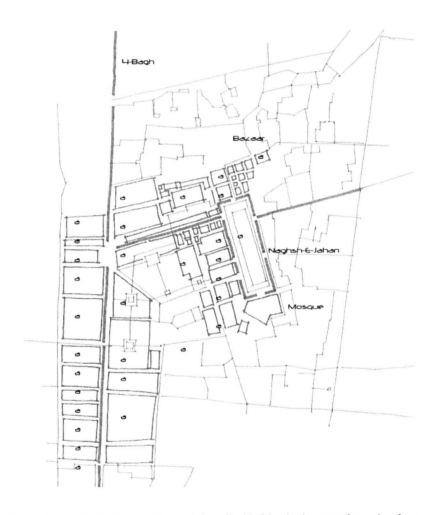

Figure 39. Applied patterns with special applicable identity in space formation from micro to macro levels.

These patterns might create actions, but will eventually settle in a balanced order. In fact space consists of fundamental units which are arranged by similar proportions that are organized into a total system. This principle, therefore, has implications on the details, as well as on their relationships, and will inherently create an overall rhythm. In contrast to these details, the viewer will create a generalized image based upon similar cases by comparing the similar mental and real concepts that he/she perceives which helps him/her categorize the subjects and apprehend the phenomena and spaces as much as possible. So space and its elements are shaped in the mind and will be recognized and evolve on the basis of pattern or patternization (Figure 40).

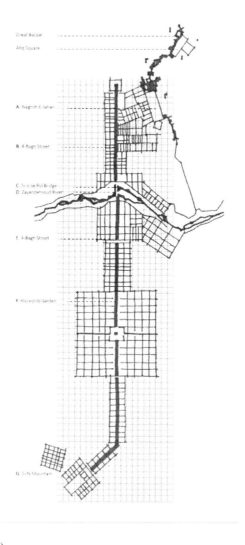

Figure 40. (Continued).

Practical Application of the Urban Design Rules and Principles 101

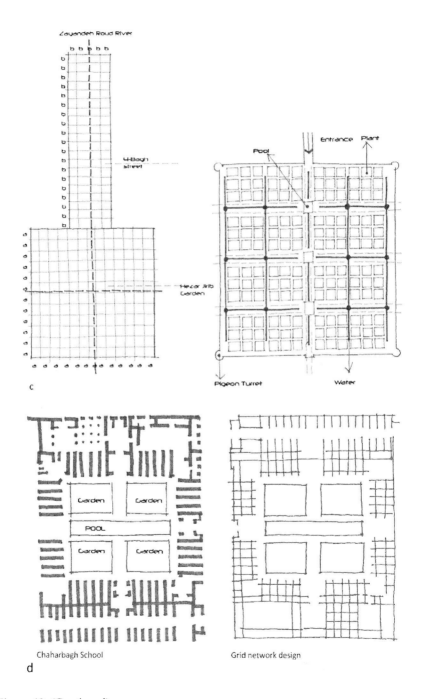

Figure 40. (Continued).

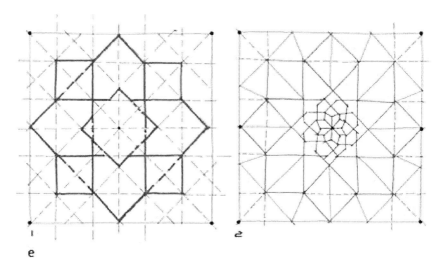

Figure 40a, b, c, d, e). Samples of the patterns applied in spaces based on practical geometry in design, their selection which was based on special guideline along with grid network. a: Urban scale (general structure), b: Urban space & Architectural scale (*Naghsh-E-Jahan* square and *Jame Abbasi* mosque) c: Urban space scale (*Chaharbagh* & *Hezarjirib* garden) d: Architectural scale (*Chaharbagh* school) e: Micro scale (Detail in tiling of *Jame Abbasi* mosque).

Spaces with similar patterns will provide the viewer with a comprehensible quality, which is the product of a distinct order in the total design (Figure 32). This order does not imply a sole and rigid repetition of elements and design factors. As we can see in the design of *Naghshe Jahan Square,* a variety of repeating forms, shapes and lines are organized in the design in a coordinated and similar, but diversified manner, and create comprehensible and long lasting forms. The result is a functional structure and an ideal form with a rational coordination and order. In fact, in the design of this space and the fundamental theory of repetition, the valuable elements and factors, which have remained unchanged throughout time and regarded as design alphabets in each culture, are repeating. The viewer will associate this alphabet to reach better conformity and comprehension of a variety of spaces (Figure 41 and 42).

Practical Application of the Urban Design Rules and Principles 103

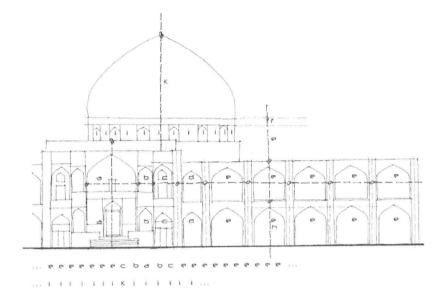

Figure 41. Meaning perception closely connected with geometrical and arithmetical proportions

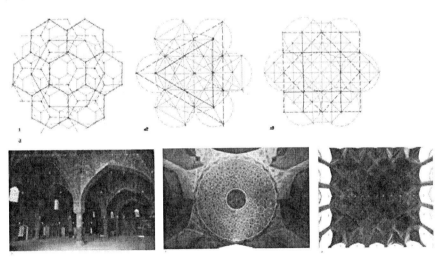

Figure 42a, b, c, d). The use and repetition of patterns in the design, structure, details and decoration of space, their ideas which are taken from nature and geometrical coordination and will help to perceive and receive meaning. (A: tile pattern in *Jame Abbasi* mosque b: *Jame Abbasi* mosque hall c: *Eslimi* pattern in the entrance ceiling d: design pattern in *Aliqapou* ceiling) (Photo by authors).

Figure 43. The elements' rhythm and repetition in the design of *bazaar* that, despite diversity in size and form, will eventually create a vast homogenous combination of forms and spaces.

The geometrical elements in *bazaar*, which have fundamental and basic units that have the potential of growth and multiplication, penetrate the fabric of the city with a diversified functional scale that has evolved through time and ultimately sustained a prolonged structure up to the current day (Figure 43).

Equilibrium Principle

The universe is composed of various units, which are recognizable and separable. Spaces are also no exception to this general rule and may be separated into fundamental units. These units differ in terms of various qualitative and quantitative characteristics such as: scale, proportion, form,

Practical Application of the Urban Design Rules and Principles 105

etc. These units are combined with each other, and since the units are not reproducible forever and therefore cannot reach a universal scale, we will reach the balance and unity of various types of these units. Composition, combination or change of scale can lead to larger spaces. When an in-depth analysis is performed on elements and basic units of design, performed with regards to the ideology applied in the design of *Nagshe Jahan* square, a specific proportion arises, $\sqrt{2}$. In all spaces the units are a factor of this number. For example, this proportion has been used and can be identified within the module or measurement of the square design and the *Shah Abbas* mosque. This is in spite of the considerable diversity in shapes and forms.

A. Gate of the Great Bazaar
B. Naghsh-E-Jahan Square
C. Palace of 40 Columns
D. Palace of Ali Qapu
E. Shaykh Lutf Allah Mosque
F. Mosque of Jame Abbasi
G. Pool Square

Figure 44. The common geometrical elements in the design of different spaces.

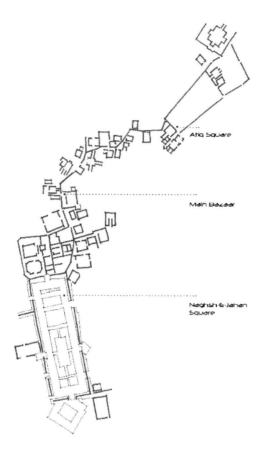

Figure 45. The design of total space is the result of a continuous system, in which each space is, in turn, independent. (Old square-*Atiq*, bazaar and *Naghsh-E Jahan* square).

Considering the cosmic pattern and natural laws which had been the source of inspiration for the designers at the time this number, that shows relationship and geometrical proportions in this space, reflects the growth process of phenomena in nature. In another words, the governing rules shaping visual factors of this space are the same as fundamental rules of growth in nature.

The eventual design of the space consists of collections of common geometrical structures and the resulted order in design is based on systematic and orderly relations (Figure 44). In fact, the design grammar and the linguistic pattern of *Nagshe Jahan* square are completed with a network of interrelated patterns of *Bazaar, Hojrehha, Saraha* and *Timche*. With the diversity of mass and semi-mass spaces, continuous, coordinated and rhythmic spaces are created.

Due to the application of quantitative proportions, the overall design benefits from total unity and integration, which in general leads to equilibrium? This equilibrium holds from micro to macro scales in both the solid and void spaces. Since, in Iranian thought, matter is the symbol of earth and substance, and void space stands for soul and sky, the designer's skill rests on striking a balance between these two dimensions. It is obvious that visualizing meaning and space soul is not possible without the existence of matter (Figure 45).

Equilibrium in this sense is a general concept, which covers this world as well as the universe. The emphasis Iranian scholars have put on equilibrium confirms that this principle implies the orderly and regularity of both man-made space and of society. Also, equilibrium is regarded as the fundamental principle of the *Ideal city* of *Farabi* and the basis of ordering and physical balance (Figure 46).

An urban form analysis in this space yields the shapes of spheres and hemispheres, rectangles, and right angles. Each stand on one of its lines, creating balance and symmetry in the space. The shapes' directions are vertical or horizontal to set balance in two directions (Figure 47).

Figure 46. Square area connects surrounding buildings to each other and plays the role of mediator and moderator (Photo by authors).

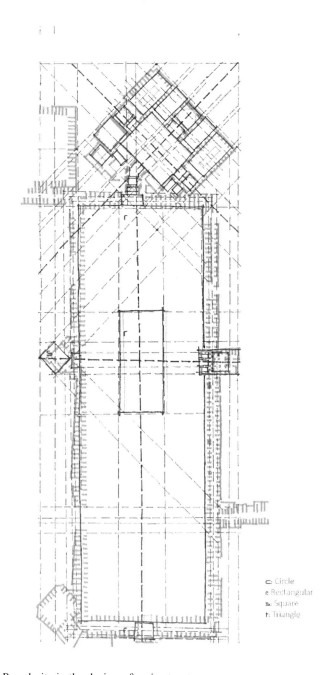

Figure 47. Regularity in the design of main structure.

Practical Application of the Urban Design Rules and Principles 109

Figure 48. Use of solid and void in ceiling of mosque (Photo by authors).

As for the combination of colors in space, a combination of warm and cold colors has been used on the façades, domes, and entrances. This combination of colors and materials lead still more balance in the space. This is the most common form of combining contrasting colors in the hot and arid climate of Iran.

Using light in the combination of void and solid of space façades creates a balanced combination of light and shadow (Figure 48 and Figure 78).

The other manifestation of balance in space is the application of proportions and how they apply to the locations of the main elements in the space of the square (Figure 49). Using a ratio of 1/3 in the overall layout of the square and the location of two spaces in the center of smaller line (i.e., *Shah Mosque* and *Gheisarieh bazaar*) and two more spaces in ⅓ square in front of each other have created a general balance. The disposition of these elements against each other has created a symmetrical space and eventually a balanced order (Figures 50 and 51).

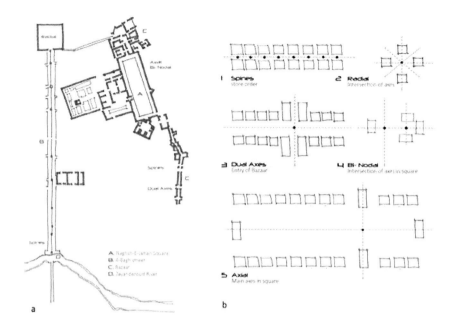

Figure 49. The principal orders and the internal relation of components in the design of space: a) order in main structure, b) different order in design).

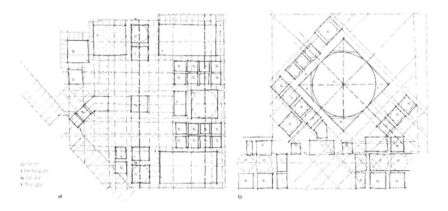

Figure 50. The dimensions and shapes used in the design of space and numerous patterns, when combined together, create total balance and cohesion. (a: *Jame Abbasi* mosque b: *Sheikhlotfolah* mosque).

Practical Application of the Urban Design Rules and Principles 111

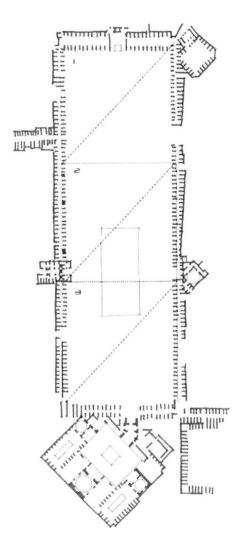

Figure 51. The use of golden ratios, basic module and its expansion in design.

CENTRALITY PRINCIPLE

In the Iranian culture this principle is so comprehensive that it includes other principles. Centrality is the symbol of unity and the foci of human worship. Regular shapes that are centered around specific points, when used in the design of spaces, is a reflection of this principle (Figures 52) and 53).

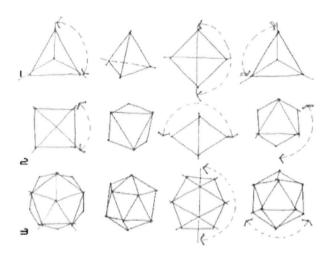

Figure 52. Geometrical analysis and the central points.

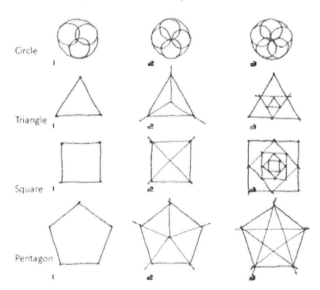

Figure 53. Design begins with Plato's forms (triangle, circle and square) and extends to complex and extensive areas in design.

Practical Application of the Urban Design Rules and Principles 113

In this ideology, sacred places are always located in the centre of universe. Their spatial totalities are ordered by or are in relation to the center. Otherwise, the spatial design will be fragmentary and disordered. In this design approach, the quality nature of forms project toward the center and, as the result of this coordination and order, orderly shapes and multiple patterns are created. This transformation may be seen in the best possible form in the design of traditional spaces where the rectangular transforms into the circular. This art is well reflected in the architecture of *Achaemenian* and *Sassanid* (Figures 54 and 55).

As time passed Iranians reached to the highest point in this skill and created masterpieces such as *Bazaar, Sheikh Lotfolah* mosque, and *Shah Mosque*. According to the centrality definitions, *Naghshe Jahan* square is located in the middle of a built up area of the city which attracts people's attention and thus became the location of various urban activities. The square has been and is regarded as the center of many activities, although geometrically it is not located exactly at the center of the city (Figure 56).

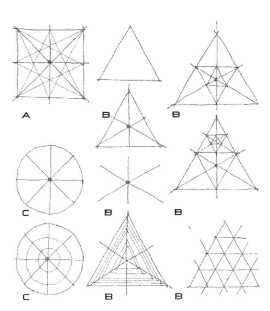

Figure 54. The principal orders of forms, on their basis which space design has been developed.

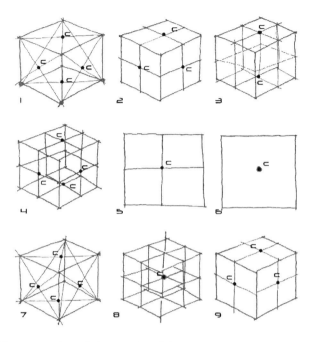

Figure 55. The conversion of plane and spatial geometry to each other on the basis of geometrical operations.

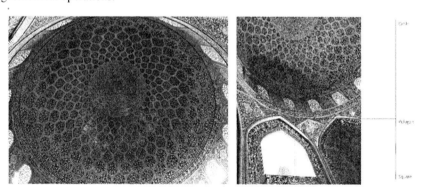

Figure 56. The geometric patterns and conversion of geometrical forms to each other that using a simple step-by step process reached its artistic climax during *Safavid* dynasty (Photo by authors).

In spite of functional differences (religious, governmental and economic) this space operates cohesively and it is the most significant factor in ordering the city structure and texture. Also, the square provides

Practical Application of the Urban Design Rules and Principles 115

legibility and identity for the city. So it is regarded as the center from the formal, symbolic and functional aspects (Figure 57).

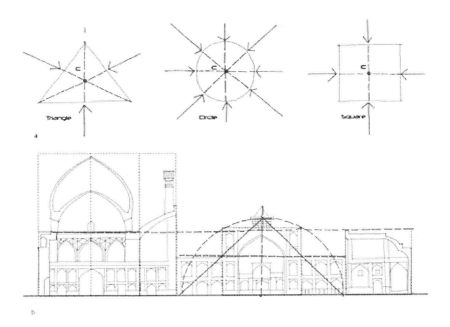

Figure 57a, b). The detailed motif system is used in all dimensions and aspects of design, (from plan to façade, ceiling, and vault), in the space design and decoration. (a: words b: sentence).

As far as form, voids and solids, in the square is concerned; there are solid and built forms on all sides, and the void is in the center, with a large pond as a symbolic element that accentuates the center. The pond is situated in a way to reflect the main elements around the square (Figure 58).

At the architecture scale, central court form has been used in the design of mosques, which is one of the main characteristics of architecture in the hot and arid climate due to both climatic considerations and its ability to capture the benefit of sunlight (Figures 61 and 62). In fact the court, as a turning point at the center, is encircled by the surrounding buildings (Figures 63 and 64).

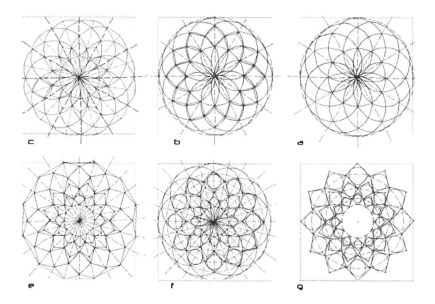

Figure 58. Radial divisions for the decoration of vaults and for the ordering of center-based spaces. (*Sheikh lotfolah* mosque). As it was mentioned before in the photography technique performed in *Naghshe Jahan* square, the viewers chose the direction of the *Shah mosque*, which reveals the main direction and centrality of this space. This is because in the definition of centrality, being in the center of attention is also important (Figures 59 and 60).

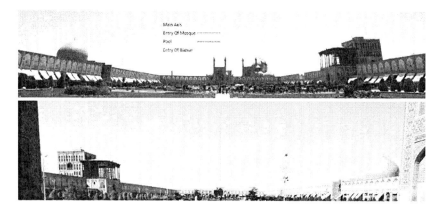

Figure 59. Application of geometrical principle by focusing on important design points and spaces along the central corridor (Photo by authors).

Practical Application of the Urban Design Rules and Principles 117

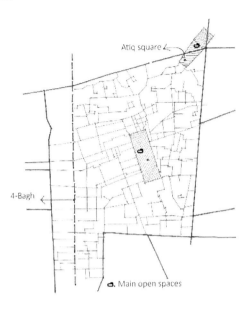

Figure 60. The dominance of abstract logic of geometry in the totality of space and the centrality of *Naghshe Jahan* square.

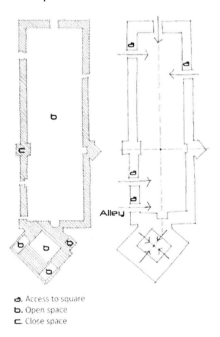

Figure 61. Mutual communicative order of form and space in design which is based on cohesion and geometrical centrality.

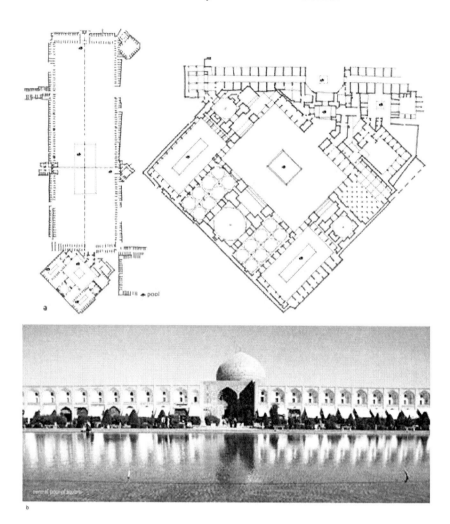

Figure 62a, b, c). The use of symbolic elements in the center, which is a unifying force in design (a: *Naghshe Jahan* square and *Jame Abbasi* mosque b: *Sheikhlotfolah* mosque) (Photo by authors).

In the internal spaces, as it was mentioned before, vaulted form is used. This form is created by transforming square into circle. Sometimes, at the center of the vault, light absorbents (skylight) are provided, which also, aside from functional role in the Iranian architecture, play a symbolic role. This reflects the belief in light and illumination at the central and elevated point of space. These skylights are also used in *Bazaar*, which, in addition

Practical Application of the Urban Design Rules and Principles 119

to ventilation and illumination, provide continuity and cohesion to show movement and circulation in the space to encourage users to move on. (Figures 65 and 66).

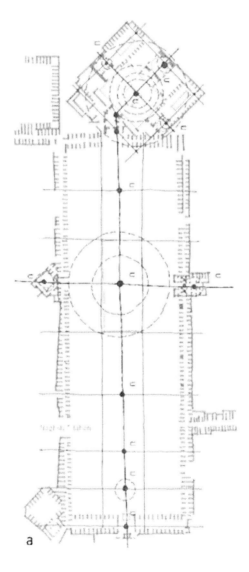

Figure 63a, b, c). Locating the principal elements in the main axes, as one of the main architectural characteristics of *Safavid* dynasty, will be clearly seen in *Naghshe Jahan* square, a) *Naghshe Jahan* square, b) & c) Jame *Abbasi* mosque (photo by authors).

Figure 64. The design method and development of geometrical patterns in the decoration.

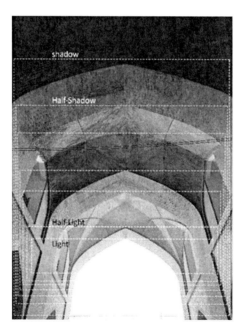

Figure 65. Using light in the direction of the main corridor, which by implying direction emphasizes movement and circulation in space (Photo by authors).

Practical Application of the Urban Design Rules and Principles 121

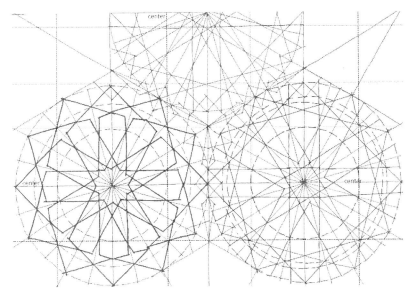

Figure 66. Repetition of centralized patterns (including main elements and their components).

Figure 67. Main transportation route and the use of light in the central corridor (Photo by authors).

So the centrality order in this space is, in fact, also the creator and perpetuator of relationships, movements and activities. In *Bazaar*, after passing through the main axis which makes its main structure, we are directed toward centers of economic activity which are called *Timche* or

Sara. These spaces, with a court at the center and a special vaulted roof, are examples of the center-oriented architecture (Figure 67).

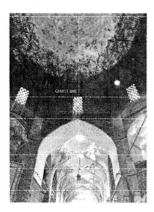 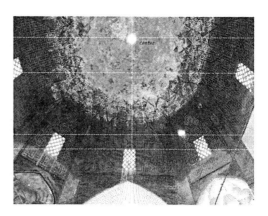

Figure 68. Use of light in the centralized design of ceilings, in which different patterns in the center and different sides are, repeated (Photo by authors).

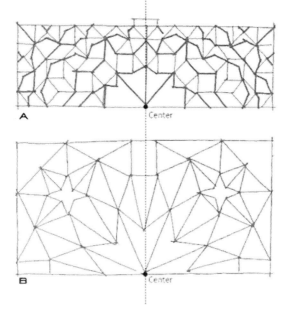

Figure 69. Combined patterns in building decoration, using radial-geometrical design.

Practical Application of the Urban Design Rules and Principles 123

Use of the centrality principle is also visible on the square façades especially on the northern and southern sides. In the design of the details and ornamentation of buildings around the square, centrality is used from the micro to the macro scale, which provides order for the design (see Figures 59 and 69).

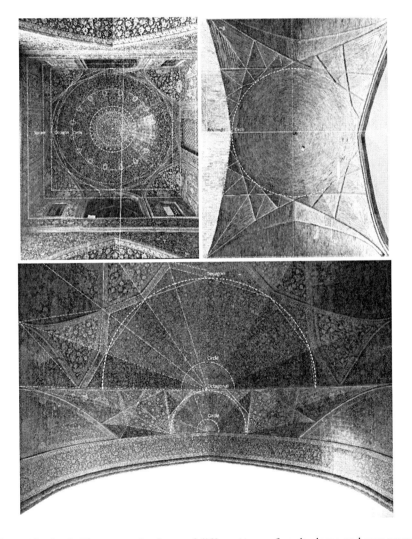

Figure 70a, b, c). The area and volume of different type of vault, dome and *muqarnas*, their design principles which are based on careful and simple calculation of forms and geometrical proportions (Photo by authors).

In these examples, in addition to order, the arrangement of lines is situated in a way that focuses onto one point, which usually stands at the center of the picture. In fact, the direction of the lines and their confluence at one specific point will direct the eyes toward that point and place emphasis on it.

In fact, focusing on certain points of space using elements like ponds, or design techniques such as *Muqarnas*[1], *Squinches*[2], *Pendentives*[3], and skylights have been common in the Iranian design in the past. These were to show the significance of these points in space. The patterns under the dome direct the eyes toward a unique point in the middle which shows the importance of centrality. The opening of this space through the area and height reinforce the idea of centrality (Figure 70).

Using a dome is, in fact, an example of central organization which creates a balanced and center-oriented configuration. In this organization the form of the central space is unifying and ordering, and it integrates the rest of less important spaces around it.

SEMANTIC AND METAPHOR

Symbolism is one of the important and prominent principles in Eastern thought and Iranian culture. Symbols convey concepts and meanings beyond the apparent, establishing precedence over reason and wisdom in order to connect to the deeper layers of humans, eventually assisting in their growth and evolution. Therefore, the designer's skill rests on recognition of this conceptual and symbolic language and to direct and guide the viewer on this basis, so that the viewer uses his/her imagination to view and perceive these concepts in space and interact with the space

---

[1] The *muqarnas* is a form that embodies the ideals of Islamic civilization: its physical form, characterized by fluidity and replication, is based as much on Islamic theological principles as it is on the more mundane principles of structural engineering.

[2] *Squinch* in architecture is a construction filling in the upper angles of a square room so as to form a base to receive an octagonal or spherical dome. Another solution to this structural problem was provided by the pendentive.

[3] Pendentive is a constructive device permitting the placing of a circular dome over a square room or an elliptical dome over a rectangular room.

according to his/her own preferences. This way, the viewer will make the space elements and factors activated and dynamic. So symbolism, or the hidden denotation in design, has the liveliness and ability to move toward the natural and instinctive state of the fixed elements and components in the design. It will eventually reach a unity in space though movement and a balanced and orderly rhythm which will last throughout time (Figure 71).

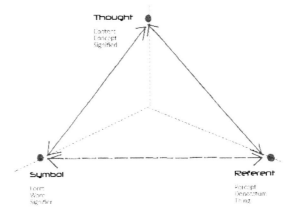

Figure 71. Triangle of reference (triangle of meaning).

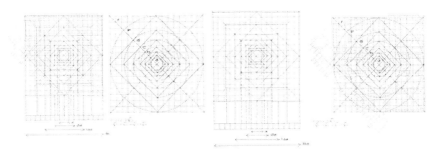

Figure 72a, b, c, d). The growth law in design is based on $\sqrt{2}$ ratio which is used in certain dimensions between spaces, and determining their distances in detail as well as the total building (Kamyar, 2015).

Numbers and proportions used in the design of *Naghshe Jahan* square and its main elements, and also the application of geometry due to its abstract forms, can take the viewer to infinity in concepts, meaning and symbols. Therefore in the Iranian culture, numbers and patterns, in addition to their functional, structural and aesthetic role, play a sacred role too. In fact, a flexible combination of mathematics and philosophy creates truth, existence, and reality in the viewer's perception (Figures 72 and 73).

Space design, on the basis of design metaphor, is not solely physical but also qualitative and symbolic, which reveals mysterious meanings and concepts. Therefore design, from micro to macro scales, conveys hidden mysteries for each group of people, culture and nation through color, shape and form. Sometimes a deeper relation of these concepts with innate human aspects leads every viewer, beyond the culture, to reflection, as it happens in the case of *Naghshe Jahan* square or *Shah Mosque*. In these cases the physical features of spaces do not just create a visual joy that is easily interpretable, but rather the viewer will interpret the visual patterns through deliberation, contemplation and reasoning. Therefore, the role of form and physical entities is the transfer of meaning. This is the same as the sacred geometry and creation of quality place.

With regard to the *Shah mosque*, Stierlin (1971) states that the current traditions in the design and structure of this mosque (of which the *Safavid* government wished to be a manifestation of resurrection) is full of hidden music, science, and mathematics. These features are only identified by the viewer through thought and contemplation.

Jung (2012) also states in this regard that the design of human thought, like instinct, is innate and hereditable, and that ancient patterns or symbols, if used properly, will act on all humans equally. The emotional and functional phenomena that reflect these thoughts function the same way everywhere; their general design is collective; their destination is the same. This, of course, should not be considered as a conflict with localization, which is based on the local values, as potentials, as well as constraints.

Unfortunately in recent designs, formalism has abolished the application of symbolism and metaphysical concepts to a large extent. But in the design of past spaces, for example the case study, the use of symbolism is quite evident. There needs to be balance between the "complete abstract" pole, i.e., metaphors, and "complete realism" pole, i.e., reason.

Practical Application of the Urban Design Rules and Principles 127

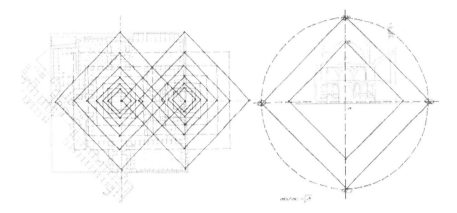

Figure 73a, b). Using basic design module will help the viewers who are viewing the space to better receive and perceive the environment and make it meaningful for them; in fact geometry make a basis for creating the logic of meaning in space.(Kamyar,2015).

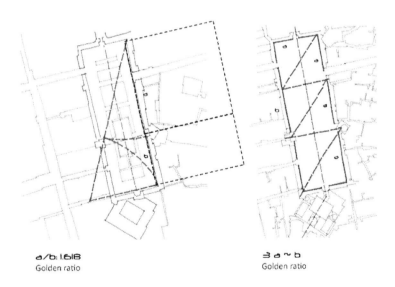

a/b: 1.618
Golden ratio

3 a ~ b
Golden ratio

Figure 74. The use of golden ratios in square.

Therefore, the mass geometry and the decomposition and composition of shapes are connected to their metaphorical and symbolic meanings. In the succeeding section, some concepts in relation to the fundamental and principal shapes in the design of *Naghshe Jahan* square will be discussed. These shapes and the Euclidian geometry give order to the space, on one hand, and are evidence of evolution and the complete order of existence, on the other. This is the main goal of art in Eastern Philosophy—conformity and compatibility with cosmic rhythm. Due to the meaning burden of the space, the vocabulary or design units will be discussed first (Figure 74).

Square

The main shape of the *Naghshe Jahan* square and surrounding spaces are based on three squares or one rectangle with a ratio of 1 to 3 (Figure 67). Square is a symbol of unity. For Plato, square is the basis and generator of coordination and justice, of which justice is the highest virtue. One can look at square to lead to the truth. This shape has the utmost stability and stasis, which in Eastern culture and tradition square is a symbol of earth and the four cardinal points. These points generate actions by making people to see and perceive during time. People's duty is to combine and make balance between four cardinal points (Figure 75).

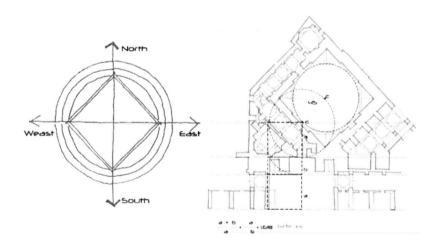

Figure 75. Combination of similar forms with different angles for design considerations creates complexity and diversity in space. Designers have used this concept in different occasions and as needed.

Practical Application of the Urban Design Rules and Principles 129

Circle

As it was stated earlier, another distinct shape used in the design of the main elements of the *Naghshe Jahan* square is circle (Figure 76).

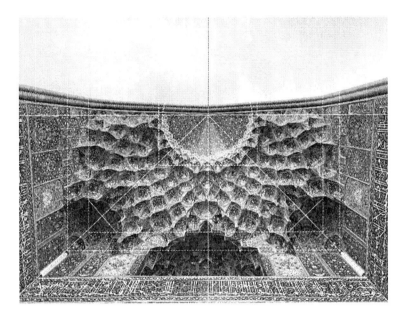

Figure 76. Geometrical forms act as the intermediate components between two original forms in design; i.e., square and circle (Photo by authors).

In historic design, the eternal point from which existence was created could be reflected in a circle, which is a symbol of cyclical and continuous movement of sky and is connected to divinity and origin. In the center of this shape all the radii are gathered in a harmonious manner to include all of the lines which start from a common point and move toward the outer edges in a coordinated way. The integrity and cohesion of lines reach its highest perfection at this central point. It is a symbol of the last stage of internal evolution or spiritual coordination. In this spherical form all lines are directed toward the center, from where their existence is realized. The cyclical movement is evolutionary and unchangeable, without a beginning and end. That is why circle is also the symbol of time which continues constantly.

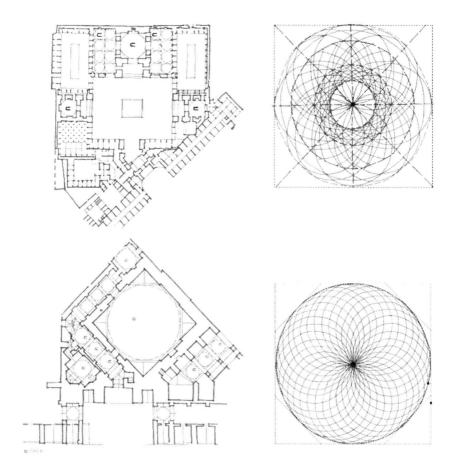

Figure 77. Geometrical pictures of concentric circles which make ordering lines, interdependent, and make complex and integrative geometry of the dome.

This form, in addition to heavenly and cosmic symbols, at a higher level is a symbol of a spiritual and transcendent world in the Eastern and Iranian philosophy (Figure 77).

Form Configuration

The combination of square and circle, which is the result of their interaction in the past art of *Mandela,* is the symbol of integrity and

Practical Application of the Urban Design Rules and Principles 131

represents a general unity that governs the universe. This is eternal and permanent. In fact, *Mandela* has been the fundamental design of religious buildings in most civilizations. As stated earlier, this combination of circle and square has been applied in various spaces such as the making of mosques and *bazaar* in and around the *Naghshe Jahan* square. Through beehive like *Goshebandi* the elements are connected which, based on symbolic concepts, are a reflection of divine movement on Earth's orders (Figures 78 and 79).

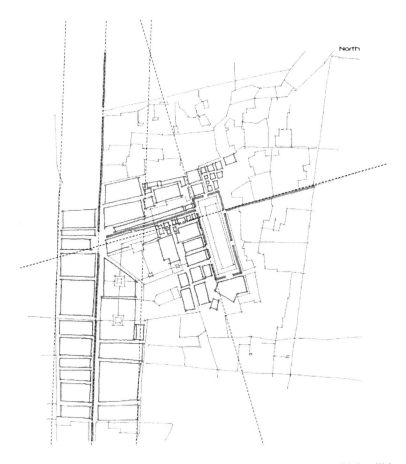

Figure 78. The main lines are located under the design infrastructure, which will lead to stronger relation between the components and the whole, and will be considered as the main elements of organizing space.

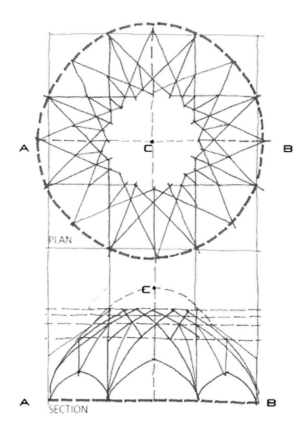

Figure 79. Geometrical growth system of forms in the plan and section of dome design, which is shaped on the basis of an original design system (basic grid pattern).

Curved Lines and *Eslimi* Design (Details)

Eslimi patterns, which have been used in the tiles of the interior of *Abbasid Jame* mosque and *Sheikh Lotfolah* mosque with rhythmic and harmonic cohesion, are nature's symbols. The basis of *Eslimi patterns*, in addition to the lines, is also the void between them, which are just as important as the main lines. These forms are created by combining regular forms, repeating them proportionally on the surface, and ultimately creating complex patterns of lines. These patterns are constantly extended; creating a symbol of immense and balanced existence which moves the

Practical Application of the Urban Design Rules and Principles 133

viewer eyes on the surface. Eventually the patterns reach a special harmony which is the reflection of total unity and oneness of the creator (Figure 80).

Figure 80. The use of void and mass in *Eslimi* design and creation of geometrical patterns in space decoration (Photo by authors).

Using Water in Design

In mysterious tradition, water is regarded as a symbol of "new birth" or re-creation, because the creation of universe is attributed to water and water is the source of life. Water is, therefore, the potential origin and the basis for universe manifestation. Application of this element may be seen at the center of *Naghshe Jahan* square and *Abbasid Jame* mosque, and also at the mosque entrance, in the smaller courtyards, and at the entrance of the *Gheisarieh* bazaar (Figure 81).

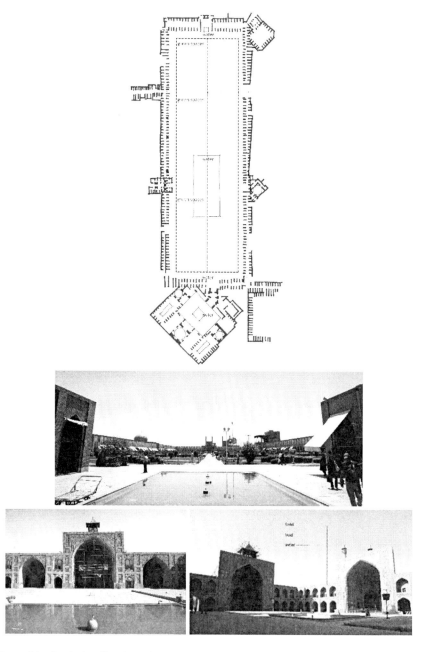

Figure 81a, b, c). Application of water and plant and the natural order at the intersection of main corridors of the square (Photo by authors).

Using Light in Design

In the Eastern philosophy, light is considered as the manifestation of illumination and divinity, which sends out darkness and dullness and turns them into existence. Light is the principal symbol for unity. Although light itself may not be seen, by shining on surfaces and thus breaking down into different colors light becomes visible. The role of the designer is to use light; collect and disperse it in space in order to create a contrast with darkness and embark on artistic creation (Figure 82).

Figure 82a, b). Symbolic application of the light and shadow contrast which creates a kind of continuity of meaning in design (*Bazaar*) (Photo by authors).

Using Plants

Nature has had a deep-rooted connection with people's lives in Iran, and is considered a fundamental element of life. Plants have always been the symbol of greenness, joy and beauty. These symbols of plants, in addition to climatic considerations in the hot and arid areas of desert, make plants themselves a manifestation of paradise or eternal gardens.

Figure 83a, b, c). Symbolic application of the plants in domes, minarets and facade of *Jame Abbasi* mosque (Photo by authors).

Practical Application of the Urban Design Rules and Principles 137

The application of plants' patterns in spacial decoration, *Eslimis,* and tiling is also quite evident, reflecting the significance of this element in their lives (Figure 83).

CULTURE AND CONTEXT (LOCALIZATION)

To comprehend traditional concepts in architecture and urban planning one needs to grasp the special cultural views in which these concepts have been created. Because knowing the history alone or the quantitative aspects of transition and evolution, we can only reach a transient knowledge about one of the aspects and its manifestations. Traditional societies, due to their beliefs in spiritual order in addition to physical needs, demand harmony and proportion, quantitatively and qualitatively. Spaces often benefit from thorough, comprehensive and total ideology and views, based on the local beliefs, traditions and ideas, and then they are directed toward eternity. Varieties of spaces are united through common alphabets and words in design (Figure 75).

In this way, design on the basis of context or culture should be regarded as a requirement for any nation or group. Because, as stated earlier, most of the design concepts, meanings and attributes have been shaped and developed through on the basis of a special language of the same culture. To relate the viewer, designer and space together, knowing the cultural background seems necessary. For example, Iranian design language, which is rooted in Iranian cultural, social and value characteristics, includes vocabularies such as mosque, *Tekieh, Gozar, bazaar,* etc. The governing principles and design, such as centrality, hierarchy, privacy, unity, etc. regulate the relationship between these elements. This shared language of space design and physical environment is therefore quite essential. As time passes, despite the evolution of building materials and physical characteristics, the concepts in this shared language become richer and stronger.

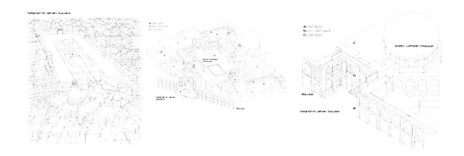

Figure 84a, b, c). Overall unity in cohesive and continuous spatial structure of square and its surrounding which has been created by using design principles and the governing relations. These design concepts and geometrical principles are applied in design, both in macro and micro levels.

The square, as a main element, has a strong relationship with its surrounding which, when viewed with its surroundings and within the general structure of the city, is perceived as a cohesive whole. In this regard, details based on Iranian culture are used at the urban, as well as architectural scales. At each scale it is complete, per-se, and is conforming to its context. So this space talks to its viewers with a familiar language and expression and establishes a strong and reciprocal relationship which provides identity and evolution.

Also at the architectural scale of *Abbasid Jame* mosque, one can see the design elements and attributes that are the most complete examples of Iranian design words and grammar:

1. "Using combined shapes to create the general geometrical shape (composition) (Figure 78 a);
2. Using orthogonal shape (purity of shape and form) (Figure 78b);
3. Inclination to use complete geometrical shapes (aesthetics);
4. Using square or rectangle in open space (Function) (Figure 78c);
5. Using a combination of open, closed and semi-open spaces (Continuity-Hierarchy) (Figure 78d);
6. Using water in open spaces (semantic-order);
7. To extend buildings toward Mecca (*Qebleh*)(Philosophy-metaphor);

Practical Application of the Urban Design Rules and Principles 139

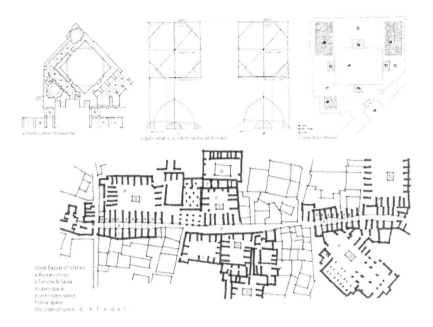

d: continuity and Hierarchy in open, semi open and close space, bazaar of Isfahan

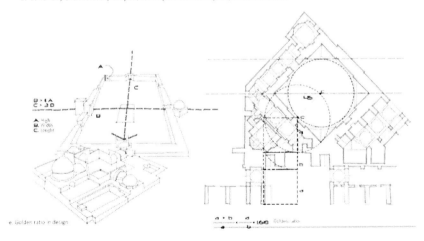

Figure 85a, b, c, d). Iranian design words and grammar.

8. General inclination toward the tradition of square dimensions (unity/order/metaphor);
9. A good sense of enclosure that is achieved with a mosque's height in relation to pathway width (Closure/Territories);

10. Using "a","2a" to "3a" ratios (composition) (Figure 78e);
11. Formation, orientation and adaptation of the mosque to the neighborhood fabric (Sustainability- Unity/Multiplicity)" (Habibi and Ahari, 2011) (Figure 85).

BINARY

To set values for the architectural and urban complexes in the design of past spaces, various types of contrast have been used. Examples are: void and mass; right-angled and curved; straight and angled; continuous and crisscross; smooth and coarse; dark and light; horizontal and vertical; etc.

These attributes have been used in the *Naghshe Jahan* square in the best possible form of contrast through domes, minarets, contrast in building materials; light and shade, which eventually create a rich combination. Each element has been given a distinct and unique character, which will eventually settle in a united whole. On the basis of these dichotomies, space will become dynamic. Through the unification of the contrasts these spaces become comparable, and their meanings and characteristics become richer and reflective for us. Human senses need recognition and distinction which is possible only through contrast.

The functional forces in the main elements of the square have their unique attributes and characteristics which, through their distinctness, will increase the legibility of space. Gaps, openings, mass and void, in plan and in façade, will further create a richer spatial perception. Combination of orderly design of the square with the organic, dense and compact texture of the surrounding area will make this space unique and distinct.

Other examples of contrast in this square are the reciprocal action and reaction between positive and dynamic, fragmented and negative shapes and forms. Continuous and movement distances direct the viewer toward an active action through connectivity and continuity, such as the linear bazaar path, colonnades surrounding the interior court of the mosque, or the entrance corridors in the *Sheikh lotfolah* mosque and *Aliqapo* palace,

Practical Application of the Urban Design Rules and Principles 141

which through light and shadow play, encourage the viewer to move. On the contrary, when distances become shorter and slower through geometry, scale, and openings, the viewer will be invited to rest and calm. Examples are shops, *Sarai, Timche,* mosque's *Jelow khan* (Figure 86).

Continuity and discontinuity are, therefore, other concepts of contrast used in this space. These spatial contrasts of close and open, light and shadow, opening and closed, and straight and torsion spaces prevent monotony and grayness, and make the environment pleasant. Putting more emphasis on certain design factors through the creation of contrast with other elements of context and environment leads to their distinction and thereby, attracts viewers' eyes. Unique and special elements will be more effectively perceived and recorded and lead to better legibility, attraction and movement in space. This is the same unique characteristic of landmarks which, in contrast to other elements, create a unique image. Examples are the contrast seen in the scale and height of the Shah mosque and other elements on the edges, or the orientation of the mosque in the totality of the square space. So the repetition of differences and dualities along a path or space lead to desired continuity and diversity, which will be further enriched by being complimented with different functions (Figure 87).

Figure 86a, b, c). The light and shadow contrast.

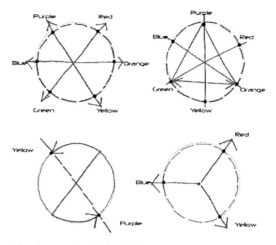

The colors opposite each other had the strongest contrast and harmony

Figure 87. The colors wheel and colors opposite.

Figure 88. The common geometrical structure despite difference in dimensions and shapes.

Also, color contrast in the design of *Naghshe Jahan* square creates visual richness and diversity. This contrast or diversity may be attributed to

Practical Application of the Urban Design Rules and Principles 143

the use of cold colors such as blue-turquoise or *Parsee* green in combination with warm ones such as yellow and cream on the facades and main facings, of which the colors themselves are the main factors to distinguish elements from each other.

Aside from color contrasts, using light and shadow on the facades and internal spaces is also quite evident. This will cause more sensibility of sensory forces and a better perception of surfaces and masses. As Robert Venturi (2007) puts it "simultaneous perception of the combination of different surfaces causes hesitation in the viewer which completes his/her perception."

So light intensity or weakness are strengthening or weakening factors of an aspect. According to Eastern ideology, light, which is the symbol of illumination and virtue, in the most sacred spaces and in the buildings' peaks is shown with more intensity (Figures 88 and 89).

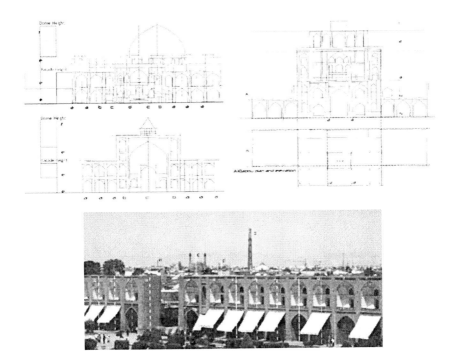

Figure 89. Contrast in height (as the main point of design).

UNITY-MULTIPLICITY

Different components in space design can, at the same time that each element is complete and solved such as main elements (*Naghshe Jahan* square, *Gheisarieh* bazaar, *Ali Qapou* palace, *sheikh Lotfolah* mosque, and Shah mosque), be combined with each other to make a whole which in itself is complete. This principle is discussed here under unity-multiplicity (Figure 90).

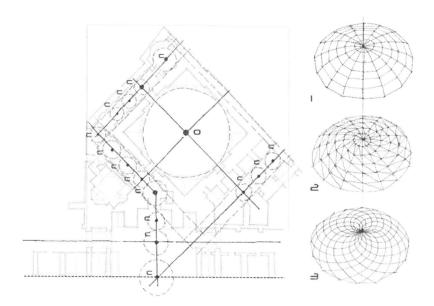

Figure 90. Space formation on the basis of systematic and orderly relations, from micro to macro levels.

As it was stated earlier, believing in unity and oneness of the universe, creator and the creation of the united and coordinated order, and cohesion of existence components, are all the basis of this principle. So although each individual design element and space is purposeful, it is the general configuration that establishes the connection and cohesion among these elements and spaces. This configuration, like an invisible order, causes unity on the whole, thereby implying uniformity and sameness of the component units. During the modern era, this unity was baseless and was shown only through superficial similarities. While this connection takes place in design through unique fundamental concepts and meanings (Figure 91).

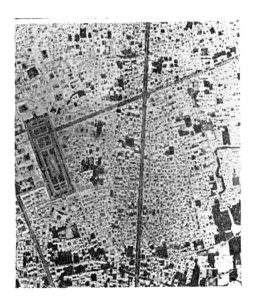

Figure 91. The connectivity between the components and the main elements of surrounding is set through the square, and in spite of differences and the diversity of types create an overall unity through a predictable order. (Iran Cartographic Center, Isfahan 1956).

The fundamental units in design create patterns. These patterns generate shapes and have the power of creating infinite plurality. These patterns are organized in the appropriate structure and hierarchy, which will eventually lead to a cohesive and unique whole (Figure 92). In the traditionalist view, unity may occur in three ways:

1. "Geometry, which manifests unity in spatial order.
2. Weight, which reflects unity in the indirect and physical order of space.
3. Light, which signals united and infinite meaning through shapes" (Burckhardt, 2009).

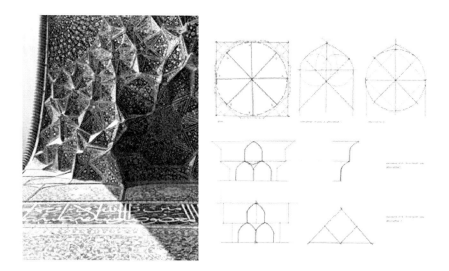

Figure 92a, b). Artistic and beautiful visual structure on the basis of transparency principle (reducing the matter and material and increasing empty space, which by breaking light and shadow infuse meaning to the viewer) (Photo by authors).

In the design of urban spaces of *Naghshe Jahan* square, spaces are expanded infinitely through elements and variety of geometrical components. *Bazaar*, which begins from the surrounding main elements of space, (*Ali Qapou* palace, *Shah* mosque, and *Sheikhlotfolah* mosque) moves toward *Jame* mosque in a cellular manner with a flexible design and a plan and spaces such as public baths, coffee shops, *saras*, etc. that are built around it. Open courtyards like textured lungs play the role of breathing. This vital shape in its totality reflects religious, political, economic and social unity of traditional society.

In form analysis, the globe, in Eastern ideology, is the most obvious mystery and analogy of unity, which when divided into regular polygons constitutes the foundation and basis of all traditional laws, coordination and order. Through the application of laws and regulations of numbers, mathematics and geometry, these shapes are produced and multiplied, and when combined, return to their original unity. Examples of these transformations may be seen in the *Gonbadkhaneh* and *Sahns* of *Jame Abbasi and Sheikh Lotfolah* mosque (Figure 93).

Practical Application of the Urban Design Rules and Principles 147

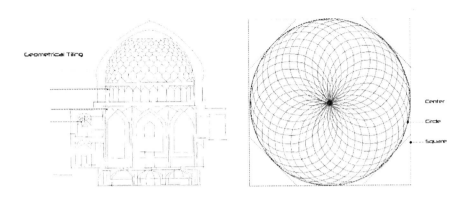

Figure 93. Diversity of form and volume production from triangle (the sequence and composition of these forms create dynamism and movement).

In another view, in design, movement of a point makes line and turning a line makes a surface, from which circles and other shapes are generated. The internal quality of a circle is unity and at the same time multiplicity. Three principal shapes are generated from circle: triangle, hexagon, and square. This attribute is clearly shown in the design of spaces (Figure 94).

Also in the Eastern and Iranian ideology, light is the symbol for unity, which when divided into colors and multiplied, becomes visible. But at the end, in spite of the perception of diversity and multiplicity of colors, the original light is united. The reason for plurality is that different forms and colors absorb and disperse the original light in various ways to benefit from the original light and, are thus, transformed (Figure 95).

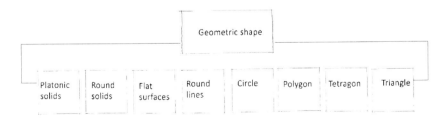

Figure 94. Form classification on the basis of geometry and eastern philosophy.

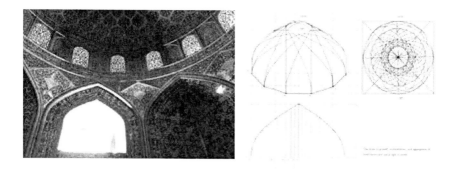

Figure 95a, b). Light the symbol of unity, *sheikh lotfolah* mosque dome and *bazaar* ceiling (Photo by authors).

Place, therefore, includes soul and mass. Although the physical and total limits are diverse and multiple, the general soul of the building or general light as the content of space remains the same, which acts as the collector and connector of various elements.

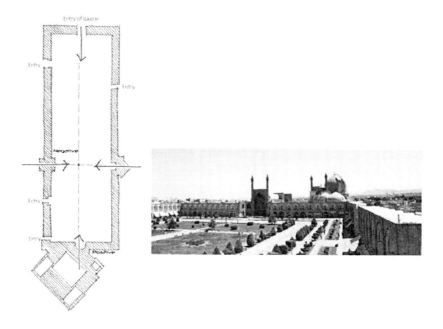

Figure 96a, b). Negative and positive form in *Naghshe Jahan* square (Photo by authors).

Practical Application of the Urban Design Rules and Principles 149

These spatial units appear in the negative and positive form, but regardless of the way they are presented their creation is both unique and the same; it is their formal aggregate and physical manifestation that is diverse while their whole creation is unique. The multiplicity of elements in the form of material is the result of the degree with which they benefit from the original source. These diverse and multiplied forms try to express unified values and meanings, which is so skillfully reflected in the *Naghshe Jahan* square so that the whole space looks one and integrated. This is because it has been built in a coordinated and harmonic manner, which is due to the total spirit of the place and its total unity, which could be attributed to three different orders in design, i.e., natural order, geometrical order and harmonic order. General unity in the architecture of hot and arid regions takes place through formation of various elements around the central court. This can be also seen in the design of *Naghshe Jahan* square and the surrounding elements (Figure 96).

This coordination is like music, so that although many notes play a role to create a piece, but the final melody is perceived on the basis of general unity and cohesion between them. Space too is shaped by general combination of elements to become an integrated collection (Figure 97).

Figure 97a, b). Creating appropriate rhythm and pulse in design by using growth and succession of proportions and the fundamental module (photo by authors).

The design principles represent *how the designer uses the alphabets and elements* to create the "place." And these principles can be used to evolve public spaces into "public places (For more examples see Figures 98 to 100, two historical squares in Iran).

Figure 98a, b, c, d). *Amir Chakhmaq* Complex.

Practical Application of the Urban Design Rules and Principles 151

Figure 99a, b). *Ganjali Khan* Complex.

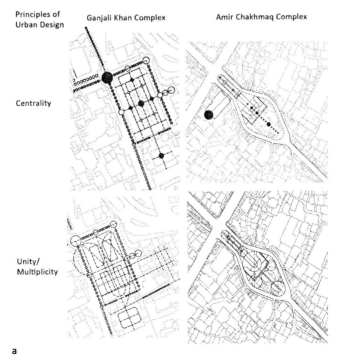

a

Figure 100 (Continued).

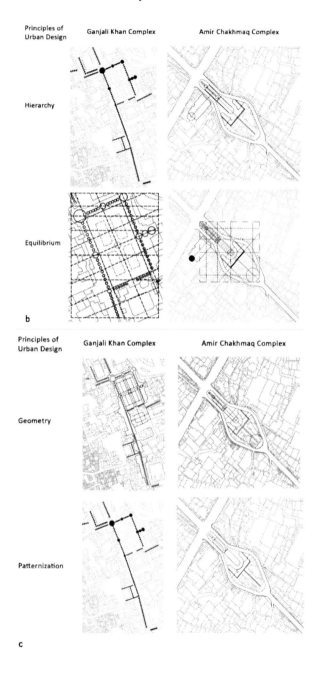

Figure 100a, b, c). Principles of Urban Design in *Ganjali Khan* Complex and *Amir Chakhmaq* Complex.

SUMMARY

There is ample evidence today to show that man, from the beginning of civilization and throughout history, has sought to gain some kind of control and impose some sort of order on his/her physical environment. Although these general goals of control and order have basically remained the same in time, their meanings, interpretations and means through which control and order are attained, have been constantly changing. In every period of history, the needs, preferences and aspirations of a society have been the determinant factors that defined and specified the means to and ends of those general goals. The Industrial Revolution brought about a turning point in the nature of the means and ends pursued in urban design. The traditional artifact gave way to the giant megalopolis: the artistic subject of civic design was transformed into the scientific area of urban design and city planning; and the purpose of designing cities changed from magnificent levels of achievement and artistry to practical efficiency, comfort and justice in the cities. Today the subject matter of urban design includes form as well as function, aesthetics as well as efficiency and process as well as product. The means to these ends have to be also modified accordingly.

The knowledge base of urban design contains the means for achieving the established goals. Recognition of this knowledge base and its components seems to be a significant step toward a better understanding of the ends, the means and means-ends relationship in urban design.

Following a brief review of the integrative theory and language of urban design, the book focuses on the theory-practice relation in urban design (see Chapter Four) which is still one of the significant, but the same time, unresolved problems in urban design. The core of the book is Chapter Five, where the practical application of the integrative urban design rules and principles is illustrated through documentation and analysis of a real-world urban design project in the historical section of the city of Isfahan, Iran. Our premise here is that this is not only a test for the applicability of the suggested urban design rules and principles, but also a method that makes it possible to learn some new and meaningful ideas through documentation and analysis of the past experiences.

REFERENCES

Abaza, H., and A. Baranzini. (2002). *Implementing sustainable development: Integrated Assessment and participatory decision-making processes*. United Nations Environment Program (UNEP).

Abukhater Ahmed Baha' El-Deen (2009). Rethinking planning theory and practice: a glimmer of light for prospects of integrated planning to combat complex urban realities, *Theoretical and Empirical Researches in Urban Management* Number 2(11)/May 2009. Number 2(11).

Alexander, E. R. (1992). 'A Transaction-Cost Theory of Planning', *Journal of the American Planning Association* 58(2): 190–200.

Alexander, E. R. (2010). Introduction: Does planning theory affect practice, and if so, how? *Planning Theory* 2010 9: 99.

Alexander, C. (2002). The nature of order: an essay on the art of building and the nature of the universe. Book one: *The phenomenon of life*. Berkeley: The Center for Environmental Structure.

Alexander, C. (2012). *The Battle for the Life and Beauty of the Earth: A Struggle between Two World-Systems*, Oxford University Press.

Alexander, R. Ernest (2015). There is no planning—only planning practices: Notes for spatial planning theories. *Planning Theory 2016*, Vol. 15(1) 91–103.

Allmendinger, P. (2002a). *Planning Theory*. Palgrave, NY.

———. (2002b). *Towards a Post-Positivist Typology of Planning Theory Planning Theory*, 2002; 1; 77.

Arnheim, R. (2001). *Entropy and art an essay on disorder and order.* Adapted from the web version available at http://acnet.pratt.edu/arch543p readings/Arnheim. Html.

Atkinson, A. (1992). The urban bioregion as 'sustainable development paradigm.' *Third World Planning Review* 14(4): 327–354.

Audirac, I. (2002). Information technology and urban form. *Journal of Planning Literature* 17(2).

Bahrainy, H. (1995). Persian-Islamic language of urban design. In *Proceedings of the congress of the Iranian history of architecture and urbanism.* Cultural Heritage Organization of Iran, Ark Bam, Kerman, Iran, February 1995.

Bahrainy, H., and B. Aminzadeh. (2007). Autocratic urban design: the case of the Navab Regeneration Project in Central Tehran. *International Development Planning Review* 29(2).

Bahrainy, H. (1998a). *Urban space analysis and design in relation to users' behavior patterns*. Tehran: University of Tehran Press. (in Persian).

Bahrainy, H. (1998b). *Urban design process.* Tehran: University of Tehran Press. (in Persian).

Bahrainy, H. and A. H. Vahdat (2015). Self-shaping and shaping by order in two paradigms of Modernism and post-Modernism. *Journal of Environmental studies,* no. 3, vol. 40, pp. 541-558 (in Persian).

Bahrainy, H. and A. Bakhtiar. (2016). *Toward an integrative theory of urban design.* Springer.

Barnes, W. F. (2001). The challenge of implementing and sustaining high performance work system in the United States: An evolutionary analysis of I/N Tek and Kote. Doctoral dissertation: University of Notre Dame.

Barnett, J. (1974). *Urban design as public policy.* New York: Architectural Record Books.

———. (1982). *An introduction to urban design.* New York: Harper & Row.

_____. (2003). *Redesigning cities: Principles, practice, implementation.* Chicago: Planners Press.

_____. (2011). *City design, modernist, traditional, green and systems perspectives.* New York: Routledge.

Batty, M. (2012). *Building a science of cities.* Cities 29 (Supplement 1): S9–S16.

Baum, Howell. (1983). *Planners and public expectations.* Cambridge, MA: Schenkman

_____. (1986). Politics and ambivalence in planners' practice. In *Strategic perspectives on planning practice*, edited by Barry Checkoway. Lexington, MA: D. C. Heath.

_____. (1996). Practicing planning theory in a political world. In *Explorations in planning theory*, edited by Seymour Mandelbaum, Luigi Mazza, and Robert Burchell, 365-82. New Brunswick, NJ: Center for Urban Policy Research, Rutgers University.

Berg, P., and R. Dasmann. (1977). Rein habiting California. *The Ecologist* 7(10): 399–401.

Berke, P. (2016). Twenty years after Campbell's Vision: Have we achieved more sustainable cities? *Journal of the American Planning Association*, Volume 82, Issue 4.

Binder, G. (2012). Theory(izing)/practice: The model of recursive cultural adaptation, *Planning Theory*, 11(3) 221–241.

Blough, D. S. (2001). *The perception of similarity.* In R. G. Cook (Ed.). Available: pigeon.psy.tufts.edu/avc/dblough/.

Boelens, Luuk (2010). Theorizing Practice and Practicing Theory: Outlines for an Actor-Relational-Approach in Planning, *Planning Theory*, Vol. 9(1): 28–62.

Broadbent, G. 1990. *Emerging concepts in urban space design.* London: Van Nostrand Reinhold.

Brown, J. L., D. Dixon, and O. Gillham. (2009). *Urban Design for an urban century, place making for people.* New Jersey: Wiley.

Burckhardt, T. (2009). *Art of Islam: Language and Meaning.* World Wisdom, Inc.

Bull, C., et al. (2007). *Cross-cultural urban design: Global or local practice?* New York: Routledge.

Campbell, S. (1996). Green Cities, Growing Cities, Just Cities? Urban Planning and the Contradictions of Sustainable Development, *Journal of the American Planning Association*, 62 (3).

Campbell H and Marshall R (1998). Acting on principle: dilemmas in planning practice. *Planning Practice and Research* 13(2): 117–28.

Carmona, et al. (2003). The communication process. In *The urban design reader. Urban Reader Series*, ed Larice, M. and E. Macdonald (2007). New York: Routledge, pp. 479–489.

Carmona, M. (2010). Public places, urban spaces: the dimensions of urban design.

Chan, C. S. (2012). Phenomenology of rhythm in design. *Frontiers of Architectural Research*. 1. 253–258. 10.1016/j.foar.2012.06.003.

Castells, M. (2000). Grassrooting the space of flows. In *Cities and telecommunications age—The fracturing of geographies*, ed. Wheeler, J. O. New York: Routledge, pp. 18–27.

Ching, F. D. K. (1979). *Architecture: Form, Space & Order*. Van Nostrand Reinhold Co, New York.

Crookston, M. (1996). Urban design and urban economics: just good friends? *Built Environment* 22(4): 300–305.

Cuthbert, A. (2006). *The Form of Cities: Political Economy and Urban Design* (Malden, MA: Blackwell Publishing).

Cuthberth, A. R. (2007). Urban design: requiem for an era review and critique of the last 50 years. *Urban Design International* 12: 177–223.

Cuthbert, A. (2011). *Understanding cities*. London: Routledge.

Dandekar, C. Hemalata (2018). Delineating the Shape of Planning Practice: John Friedmann's Legacy, *Journal of the American Planning Association* 84:2, 193-197.

Davis, M., 2006. *Planet of Slums*. Verso.

Davoudi S and Pendlebury J (2010). The evolution of planning as an academic discipline. *Town Planning Review* 81(6): 613–45.

Davoudi, S. (2015). Research impact: Should the sky be the limit? In: Silva E, Healey P, Harris N, et al. (eds) *The Routledge Handbook of Planning Research Methods*. London: Routledge, 405–413.

DeChiara, J., and L. Koppelman. (1982). *Urban planning and design criteria*, 3rd ed. New York: Van Nostrand Reinhold Company.

Dobbins, M. 2009. Cited in Brown, L. J. et al. (2009). *Urban design for an urban century, placemaking for people*. New Jersey: Wiley.

Donaghy, P. K. and Hopkins, D. L. (2006). Coherentist Theories of Planning are Possible and Useful, *Planning Theory* 2006; 5; 173.

Durning, B. (2004). Planning Academics and Planning Practitioners: Two Tribes or a Community of Practice? *Planning, Practice & Research*, Vol. 19, No. 4, pp. 435 – 446, November 2004.

Dyckman, J. (1969). *The practical uses of planning theory*, JAIP, Sep.

Eco-Village Foundation. 1994. *Proposal prepared by the Gaia Trust*, May 1994.

Elshater M. Abeer (2015). Urban design redux: Redefining a professional practice of specialization, *Ain Shams Engineering Journal*, 6(25-39).

Evans, P. & Thomas, M. (2004)). *Exploring the elements of design*. Clinton Park, NY: Delmar Learning.

Fecht, S. 2012. Urban legend: Can city planning shed its pseudoscientific stigma? *Scientific American*.

Ferreira António (2018). Towards an Integrative Perspective: Bringing Ken Wilber's Philosophy to Planning Theory and Practice, *Planning Theory & Practice*, doi: 10.1080/14649357.2018.1496270.

Ferreira, A., Sykes, O., & Batey, P. (2009). Planning theory or planning theories? The hydra model and its implications for planning education. *Journal for Education in the Built Environment*, 4(2), 29–54.

Fischler, Ralph. (1998). Communicative planning theory and genealogical inquiry. Paper presented at the Planning Theory Conference, Oxford Brookes University, Oxford, UK.

Foucault, M., (1983) *This is Not a Pipe,* Berkeley: University of California Press.

Foucault, M., (1986) 'Of Other Spaces', *Diacritics,* 16(1):22-7.

Forester, J. (1989). *Planning in the face of power*. Berkeley: University of California Press.

_____. (2012). On the theory and practice of critical pragmatism: Deliberative practice and creative negotiations, *Planning Theory* published online 7 June 2012.

Francis, M. (1984). Mapping downtown activities. *Journal of Architectural and Planning Research* 1: 21–35.

Friedmann J. (1987). *Planning in the Public Domain*. Princeton, NJ: Princeton University Press.

_____. (2002). *The Prospect of Cities* (Minneapolis: University of Minnesota Press).

_____. (2003). Why do planning theory? *JAPA* Volume: 2 issue: 1, page(s): 7-10.

Gangwar, Gaurav & Fellow, Research & Prof, Asstt. (2017). *Principles and Applications of Geometric Proportions in Architectural Design*.

Garde, M. Ajay (2008). Innovations in Urban Design and Urban Form: The Making of Paradigms and the Implications for Public policy, *Journal of Planning Education and Research* 2008 28: 61.

Gieryn, T. F. (2000). A Space for Place in Sociology. *Annu. Rev. Sociol.* 26, 463–496.

Habibi, M and Zahra Ahari. (2011). The Language of Urban Design in historical cities, Isfahan school of thought. *Iran: Cultural research bureau*. (in Persian).

Hall, P. (1997). Modeling the post-industrial city. *Futures* 29(4/5): 311–322.

Halprin, L. (1969). *Creative process in the human-environment: The RSVP cycles*. New York: George Braziller, Inc.

Harris, B. (1960). Plan or Projection: An Examination of the Use of Models in Planning, Journal of American Institute of Planners, Volume 26, 1960 - Issue 4.

Healey, P. (1992). Planning through debate: The communicative turn in planning theory. *Town Planning Review* 63: 143–162.

_____. (2011). Foreword. In J. Friedmann, *Insurgencies: Essays in planning theory* (pp. 1–14). New York, NY: Routledge.

Hetherington, K. (1998). In Place of Geometry: The Materiality of Place. *The Sociological Review,* 45(1_suppl), 183–199.

Hillier, B., & Hanson, J. (1989). *The social logic of space.* Cambridge, Cambridge University Press.

Hillier, J. (2002). '*Mind the Gap,*' in J. Hillier and E. Rooksby (eds) *Habitus: A Sense of Place*. Aldershot: Ashgate.

Hoch, Charles (1996). A pragmatic inquiry about planning and power. In *Explorations in planning theory*, edited by Seymour Mandelbaum, Luigi Mazza, and Robert Burchell, 30-44. New Brunswick, NJ: Center for Urban Policy Research, Rutgers University.

Hull, A. (2008). Policy integration: What will it take to achieve more sustainable transport solutions in cities? *Transport Policy*, 15(2), 94–103.

Hyungun Sung, Sugie Lee, and SangHyun Cheon (2015). Operationalizing Jane Jacobs's Urban Design Theory: Empirical Verification from the Great City of Seoul, Korea. *Journal of Planning Education and Research* 2015, Vol. 35(2) 117–130.

Inam, A. (2011). From Dichotomy to Dialectic: Practicing Theory in Urban Design, *Journal of Urban Design*, Vol. 16. No. 2, 257–277, May 2011,

Innes, Judith. (1995). Planning theory's emerging paradigm: Communicative action and interactive practice. *Journal of Planning Education and Research* 14 (3): 183-89.

Jacobs, A. (1978). *Making City Planning Work.* Chicago: American Society of Planning Officials.

Jung, C, G. 2012. *Man and His Symbols*. New York: Random House Publishing Group.

Kamyar, M. (2015). *Architectural Semiotics*, Isfahan Shah Abbas mosque. Tehran: Chaharderakht publishing Co. (in Persian).

Kerry R. Brooks, Barry C. Nocks, J. Terrence Farris, & M. Grant Cunningham (2002). Teaching for Practice Implementing a Process to Integrate Work Experience in an MCRP Curriculum, *Journal of Planning Education and Research* 22:188-200.

Knorr-Cetina K (2001). Objectual practice. In: Schatzki TR, Knorr-Cetina K and von Savigny E (eds) *The Practice Turn in Contemporary Theory*. New York: Routledge, 175–188.

Krieger, Martin. (1974). Some new directions for planning theories. *Journal of the American Planning Association* 40:156-63.

Krieger, A. & Saunders, W. (Eds) (2009). *Urban Design* (Minneapolis: The University of Minnesota Press).

Kuhn, D., et al. (1988). The development of scientific thinking skills. New York: Academic Press, Inc.

Kuhn, T. S. (1962). *The structure of scientific revolutions*. Chicago: University of Chicago Press.

Kuhn, T. S. (1977). *Second thoughts on paradigms, in Suppe, F. 1977, The Structure of scientific theories*, 2nd ed. Urbana.

Krier, R. (1979). *Urban space*. New York: Rizzoli. Krier, L. 1992. Leon Krier: Architecture and urban design 1967–1992. New York: St. Martin's Press.

Liggett, Helen. (1996). Examining the planning practice conscious(ness). In *Explorations in planning theory*, edited by Seymour Mandelbaum, Luigi Mazza, and Robert Burchell, 299- 306. New Brunswick, NJ: Center for Urban Policy Research, Rutgers University.

Lang, J. (1980). The nature of theory for architecture and urban design. *Journal of Urban Design* 1(2).

Lang, J. (1987). *Creating architectural theory: The role of the behavioral sciences in environmental design*. NewYork: Van Nostrand Reinhold.

Lang, J. (ed.). (1974). Designing for human behavior: Architectural and the behavioral science. Stroudsburg: Dowden, Hutchinson and Ross.

Lang, J. (1987). *Creating Architectural Theory: The Role of the Behavioral Sciences in Environmental Design.* New York: Van Nostrand Reinhold.

Lang, J. (1994). *Urban design: The American experience*, 35–58. New York: Van Nostrand Reinhold.

Lang, J. (2006). *Urban design: A typology of procedures and products*. London: Elsevier.

Lauer, D. & Pentak, S. (1995). *Design basics*, 4th edition. Ft. Worth, TX: Harcourt Brace College Publishers.

Loukaitou-Sideris, A. & Banerjee, T. (1998). *Urban Design Downtown: Poetics and Politics of Form* (Berkeley: University of California Press).

Lynch, K. (1981). *A theory of good city form*. Cambridge Mass: MIT Press.

March A. (2010). Practicing theory: When theory affects urban planning. *Planning Theory* 9(2):108–125.

Mandelbaum, S. J. (1979). 'A Complete General Theory of Planning is Impossible,' *Policy Sciences* 11: 59–71.

Margenau, H. (1972). 'The Method of Science and the Meaning of Realty,' in his *Integrative Principles of Modern Thought*, Gordon and Breach, New York.

Marshall, T. (Ed.) (2004). *Transforming Barcelona* (London: Routledge).

Marshall, R. 2009. The elusiveness of urban design: The perpetual problem of definition and role. In *Urban design*, edited by A. Krieger and W. S. Saunders, 38-57. Minneapolis: University of Minnesota Press.

Marshall, S. (2012). Science, pseudo-science and urban design. *Urban Design International* 17: 257–271.

Mascia, L. (2018). Observation on the geometry behind the design of the 'Vitruvian man' by Leonardo da Vinci.

MacDonald Kelvin, Bishwapriya Sanyal, Mitchell Silver, Mee Kam Ng, Peter Head, Katie Williams, Vanessa Watson & Heather Campbell (2014). Challenging theory: Changing practice: Critical perspectives on the past and potential of professional planning, *Planning Theory & Practice*, 15:1, 95-122,

Moss, M. L., and A. M. Townsend. (2000). How telecommunications systems are transforming urban spaces. In *Cities in the telecommunications age—the fracturing of geographies,* ed. Wheeler, J. O., et al., pp. 31–41. New York: Routledge.

McClurg-Genevese, J. (2005). The principles of design. *Digital Web Magazine* (online). Available from: /www.digital-web.com/articles/principles_of_design/S.

Mcmanus, I. (2005). Symmetry and asymmetry in aesthetics and the arts. *European Review.* 13. 157-180. 10.1017/S1062798705000736.

Morris, C. (2011). *Signs, Language and Behavior.* Literary Licensing, LLC.

Moudon, A. Vernez. (2000). Proof of goodness: A substantive basis for New Urbanism? *Places* 13(1): 38–43.

Moudon, A. Vernez. (1992). A catholic approach to organizing what urban designers should know. *Journal of Planning Literature* 64(4): 331–349.

Moudon, Anne Vemez (2003). A Catholic approach to organizing what urban designers should know. In A. R. Cuthbert (Ed.), *Designing cities: critical readings in urban design* (pp. 362-386). Oxford: Blackwell.

Norberg-Schulz, C. (1988). *Architecture : meaning and place*: selected essays.

Orly Linovski1 and Anastasia Loukaitou-Sideris (2012). Evolution of Urban Design Plans in the United States and Canada: What Do the Plans Tell Us about Urban Design Practice? *Journal of Planning Education and Research.* 33(1) 66–82.

Ozgood, C. E., and O. Tzeng, eds. (1990). Language, meaning, and culture. *The selected papers of C. E. Ozgood.* Praeger Publishers.

Plato. (1943). *Plato's The Republic.* New York: Books, Inc.

Pizarro, R. E., L. Wei, and T. Banerjee. (2003). Agencies of globalization and third world urban form: A review. *Journal of Planning Literature* 18(2).

Polydorides, N. (1983). *Concept of Centrality in Urban Form and Structure* (European University Studies) (V. 2). Frankfurt am Main; NewYork: Lang.

Punter, J. 1999. Design guidelines in American cities: Conclusion. In *The urban design reader,* ed. Larice, M., and E. Macdonald (2007). New York: Urban Reader Series.

Raelin, J. A. (2006). Does action learning promote collaborative leadership? *Academy of Management Learning and Education,* 5(2): 152–168.

Punter, J. (2007). Developing urban design as public policy: Best practice principles for design review and development management. *Journal of Urban Design* 12 (2): 167-202.

Raelin, A. Joseph (2007). Toward an Epistemology of Practice, *Academy of Management Learning & Education*, 2007, Vol. 6, No. 4, 495–519.

Rapoport, A. (1990). *The Meaning of the Built Environment: A Nonverbal Communication Approach,* University of Arizona Press.

Rittel, H., & Webber, M. (1973). Dilemmas in a general theory of planning. *Policy Sciences,* 4, 155–169.

Rosenbloom, Sandra (2018). Introduction: John Friedmann and Links to Planning Practice, *Journal of the American Planning Association*, 84:2, 178-179.

Rudlin, D., and N. Falk. (2009). *Sustainable urban neighborhood, building the 21st century home*. Oxford: Architectural Press.

Saarikoski, Heli (2002). Naturalized Epistemology and Dilemmas of Planning Practice, *Journal of Planning Education and Research* 2002 22: 3.

Salama, A. M. (2009). Knowledge and Design: People-Environment Research for Responsive Pedagogy and Practice. *Procedia -Social and Behavioral Sciences* 49, 8-27.

Sanyal, B. (2018). A Planners' Planner: John Friedmann's Quest for a General Theory of Planning, *Journal of the American Planning Association,* 84:2, 179-191.

Sanyal, Bish (2018). A Planners' Planner: John Friedmann's Quest for a General Theory of Planning, *Journal of the American Planning Association,* 84:2, 179-191.

Shepard, R. N. (1987). Toward a universal law of generalization for psychological science. *Science,* 237, 1317-1323.

Shirvani, H. (1985). *Urban design process*, Van Nostrand Reinhold.

Schumacher, P. (2009). Parametricism: a new global style of architecture and urban design, *Architectural Design*, 79(4), pp. 14–23.

Schweitzer, A. Lisa, Eric J. Howard, & Ian Doran (2008). Planners Learning and Creating Power: A Community of Practice Approach, *Journal of Planning Education and Research* 2008 28: 50.

Smith, P. (2013). *Syntax of cities*.

Smith, R. W. (1973). A theoretical basis for participatory planning. *Public Sciences* 4: 275–295.

Soja, E. W. (1989) *Postmodern Geographies: the Reassertion of Space in Critical Social Theory*, Verso, London and New York.

Soja, E. W. (1996) *Thirdspace: Journeys to Los Angeles and Other real-and-imagined Places*, BlackwellCambridge, MA.

Southworth, M. (1989). Theory and practice of contemporary urban design: A review of urban design plans in the United States. *Town Planning Review* 60 (4): 369-402.

Sternberg, E. (2000). Integrative theory of urban design. *APA Journal, Summer*, Vol. 66, No. 3, pp. 265-278.

Steinitz, C. (2007). Meaning and the Congruence of Urban Form and Activity, *Journal of the American Institute of Planners*, 34:4, 233-248, doi: 10.1080/01944366808977812 (online).

Stierlin, H. (1971). *Iran of the master builders; 2500 years of architecture*. Geneva: Sigma Editions.

Sterrett, S. (2016). *Physically Similar Systems: A History of the Concept*.

Sydow, Jorg (2018). From dualisms to dualities: On researching creative processes in the arts and sciences. *Environment and Planning A: Economy and Space* 0(0) 1–7.

Tanke, J. (2009). *Foucault's philosophy of art: a genealogy of modernity*.

Thomas, R. (ed.). (2003). Sustainable urban design: An environmental approach. New York: Spon Presss. Tibbalds, F. 1984. Urban design—Who needs it? *Places* 1(3): 22–25.

Trieb, M. (1974). *Stadtgestaltung [Urban Design]*. Birkhäuser.

Ujang, N. (2015). The Notion of Place, Place Meaning and Identity in Urban Regeneration. *Asian Journal of Environment-Behavior Studies*. Chung-Ang University, Seoul, S. Korea, 25-27.

UN Habitat (2009). *Planning Sustainable Cities: Global Report on Human Settlements 2009* (Nairobi: United Nations Human Settlements Programme, and London: Earthscan).

Venturi, R. and Denise Scott Brown. (2007). *Architecture as signs and systems: for a mannerist time.* Belknap Press of Harvard University Press.

Waldheim, C. (Ed.) (2006). *The Landscape Urbanism Reader* (Princeton, NJ: Princeton Architectural Press).

Watson, V. (2002). Do We Learn from Planning Practice? The Contribution of the Practice Movement to Planning Theory, *Journal of Planning Education and Research* 22: 178.

Yin, Robert. (1994). *Case study research: Design and methods.* Vol. 5, Applied Social Research Methods Series. Thousand Oaks, CA: Sage.

ABOUT THE AUTHORS

Hossein Bahrainy, PhD
Professor Emeritus
Department of Urban Planning, Faculty of Fine Arts,
University of Tehran, Iran
E-mail: hbahrain@ut.ac.ir; hbahrainy@yahoo.com

Hossein Bahrainy received his PhD in Urban Design and Planning from University of Washington at Seattle, in 1980. Professor Bahrainy has been a visiting professor at Iowa State University at Ames, a visiting professor at University of Central England at Birmingham, visiting scholar at Stony Brook University at New York, and University of Washington at Seattle. Currently he is Professor Emeritus at the Faculty of Fine Arts, University of Tehran. He has focused his research, teaching, and writing and practicing on the design and planning of the built-environment. The results of his research activities have been published in numerous journal articles and several books, the most recent ones which were "Toward an Integrative Urban Design Theory" (Springer, 2016), and "Urban Village: toward a pattern for sustainable settlement" (UT Press, 2017, in Persian). He was the national director for a comprehensive international project, supported by UNDP, on seismic risk reduction, the results which published in 7 volumes. This book is, in fact, a follow up to the integrative theory book and focuses on the practical application of the proposed theory.

Ameneh Bakhtiar, PhD
Assistant Professor
Department of Architecture, Faculty of Fine Arts,
University of Tehran, Iran

Ameneh Bakhtia received her PhD from Tarbiat Modares University in Tehran and is currently an Assistant Professor with the Department of Architecture, Faculty of Fine Arts, University of Tehran. She is also an architect-urban designer, who has practiced architecture and urban design extensively. Some of her projects have won national and international prizes, including: First prize of Memar national competition for a residential apt.; short listed for the Aghakhan Prize, 2019; recognized as distinguished architect of 2019 by the Isfahan Construction Engineering Organization. She was the co-author of the book "Toward an Integrative Theory of Urban Design" (Springer, 2016), and also co-translator of the book "Evolution, Cities and Design" by Stephan Marshal, UT Press, 2015. Dr. Bakhtiar has been teaching architecture and urban design at Art University of Isfahan, and Architecture Department of the University of Tehran.

INDEX

A

Achaemenian, 113
activities, vii, xi, 10, 11, 12, 13, 14, 15, 19, 20, 29, 36, 49, 50, 53, 59, 61, 62, 70, 72, 81, 97, 113, 121, 160, 169
activity circuit, 13, 14, 76
activity patterns, 12, 13
Ali Qapou, 144, 146
analogy, 53, 56, 57, 92, 146
application, v, vii, xii, xv, xvi, xviii, 15, 17, 25, 26, 36, 37, 47, 54, 58, 59, 61, 62, 63, 72, 75, 76, 78, 89, 90, 94, 107, 109, 116, 125, 126, 133, 134, 135, 136, 137, 146, 154, 170
architecture, vii, xii, xvii, 25, 31, 36, 45, 84, 91, 94, 98, 113, 115, 118, 122, 124, 137, 149, 156, 158, 162, 164, 165, 166, 167, 170
artistic, vii, xi, 1, 7, 54, 74, 93, 114, 135, 146, 153
asymmetry, 21, 22, 164

B

bazaar, 20, 22, 44, 104, 106, 109, 131, 133, 137, 140, 144, 148
binary, 34, 35, 36, 48, 51, 140
boundaries, 29, 30, 31, 32, 33, 34, 61

C

Catholic, xiv, 7, 164
centrality, 4, 26, 27, 28, 29, 97, 111, 113, 116, 117, 121, 123, 124, 137, 164
Chaharbagh, 90, 102
circle, 112, 118, 129, 130, 147
collaborative, xvii, 68, 73, 74, 164
communicative, xvii, 77, 82, 117, 159, 160, 161
compatibility, xiii, 128
complexity, xii, xiv, 10, 11, 15, 25, 31, 50, 61, 75, 76, 83, 128
composition, 105, 127, 138, 140, 147
conceptual, v, xi, 17, 34, 42, 83, 84, 124
configuration, 90, 124, 130, 144
conformity, 102, 128
consensus, 2, 72, 73

contemporary, xii, 1, 28, 44, 70, 82, 83, 84, 85, 86, 92, 162, 166
context, xviii, 20, 45, 58, 59, 61, 76, 81, 84, 86, 87, 137, 138, 141
continuity, 2, 22, 24, 25, 26, 29, 48, 49, 119, 135, 138, 140, 141
control, xiii, 2, 14, 25, 36, 39, 47, 50, 68, 73, 77, 84, 153
convergence, xiv
creativity, 9, 76
critical theory, xii, xiii, xiv, xviii, 18, 78, 81
culture, xiv, 3, 19, 20, 50, 54, 61, 62, 70, 85, 92, 102, 111, 124, 126, 128, 137, 138, 164
cybernetics, 47, 48

D

decomposition, 127
dialogical, 5
dichotomy, xi, xiv, xvii, 6, 80, 82, 161
discipline, xi, xviii, 2, 6, 14, 48, 49, 50, 68, 158
disequilibrium, 40, 50
disorder, 48, 49, 50, 51, 52, 156
divergence, xiv
diversity, 15, 25, 31, 32, 36, 48, 49, 50, 64, 104, 105, 107, 128, 141, 142, 145, 147
domes, 109, 136, 140
dualism, 1, 3
duality, 1, 3
dynamic, 3, 9, 13, 22, 31, 36, 38, 39, 40, 43, 49, 58, 91, 93, 125, 140

E

Eastern philosophy, 135
economics, 67, 68, 158
emancipation, xiv, 77, 78
emerging paradigm, xiv, 161

environmental, xiii, xvii, 11, 26, 39, 47, 48, 49, 53, 64, 77, 155, 156, 162, 166
epistemological, xviii, 7
equilibrium, 21, 38, 39, 40, 41, 104, 107
Eslimi, 103, 132, 133
essential, 11, 17, 20, 24, 37, 39, 50, 60, 64, 70, 98, 137
Euclidian, xvii, 2, 127

F

feedback, 39, 47, 48
form, 6, 10, 11, 12, 13, 15, 20, 21, 22, 23, 25, 26, 27, 29, 31, 34, 35, 36, 39, 45, 47, 48, 49, 51, 53, 54, 55, 56, 58, 61, 62, 67, 69, 70, 71, 73, 75, 81, 82, 83, 84, 86, 87, 91, 93, 97, 102, 104, 107, 109, 113, 115, 117, 118, 124, 126, 129, 130, 138, 140, 146, 147, 148, 149, 153, 156, 158, 160, 163, 164, 166

G

General Systems Theory, 58
generic, 2, 7, 71
geometry, 45, 46, 47, 90, 97, 102, 114, 117, 125, 126, 127, 130, 141, 145, 146, 147, 161, 163
Gestalt, 59, 60
Gheisarieh, 109, 133, 144
globalization, 70, 164
golden ratios, 111, 127
Gonbadkhaneh, 146
grammar, xv, 10, 106, 138, 139
grid, 22, 102, 132

H

Habermas, 77, 78, 81, 82
hexagon, 147

Index

hierarchical, 11, 36, 37, 38
hierarchy, 29, 34, 36, 37, 50, 137, 138, 145
historical, xii, xvii, 7, 44, 71, 73, 77, 94, 150, 154, 160
human ecology, 59

I

implication, xvi, 78
innovation, 2, 9
instrumental, 6, 77, 78, 80, 82
integrative, v, vii, xi, xii, xiv, xv, xvi, xvii, xviii, 1, 2, 3, 6, 7, 8, 9, 10, 14, 15, 17, 18, 19, 75, 76, 77, 78, 82, 83, 89, 130, 154, 156, 159, 163, 166, 169, 170
intuitive, vii, xi, 10, 15, 17, 71, 74, 75, 76, 86
Isfahan, xii, xvi, 19, 90, 92, 94, 145, 154, 160, 161, 170

K

knowledge, vii, ix, xi, xiv, xvii, 2, 6, 7, 9, 10, 11, 15, 17, 18, 39, 53, 62, 68, 69, 73, 77, 78, 80, 82, 83, 85, 87, 93, 96, 137, 153, 165
knowledge base, vii, xi, 10, 15, 18, 80, 93, 153

L

language, v, ix, xi, xv, xvi, xvii, xviii, 4, 5, 9, 10, 11, 12, 13, 14, 15, 17, 18, 19, 53, 61, 62, 74, 75, 76, 81, 93, 124, 137, 138, 154, 156, 157, 160, 164
legitimacy, vii, xi
lessons, v, 89
light, 20, 21, 64, 109, 118, 120, 121, 122, 135, 140, 141, 143, 145, 146, 147, 148, 155

linguistics, xviii, 18, 81
localization, 61, 126, 137

M

man-environment, xvii, 52
Margenau, Henry, 1, 6, 9, 163
meaning, xii, xvii, 13, 14, 25, 34, 42, 44, 53, 54, 58, 59, 60, 62, 73, 77, 85, 91, 97, 103, 107, 125, 126, 127, 128, 135, 145, 146, 157, 163, 164, 165, 166
metaphor, 53, 55, 56, 57, 124, 126, 138, 139
metaphorical, 127
meta-theories, xvii, 4, 18
methods of inquiry, vii, xi, 74, 75, 77
minarets, 136, 140
module, 21, 105, 111, 127, 149
multiplicity, 48, 49, 50, 51, 140, 144, 147, 149
muqarnas, 123, 124

N

Naghshe Jahan square, 94, 113, 116, 117, 118, 119, 125, 126, 127, 128, 129, 131, 133, 140, 142, 144, 146, 148, 149
nonessential, 50
non-euclidian, 2
normativity, xii

O

order, xiv, xv, xvi, 10, 11, 13, 14, 20, 21, 22, 36, 38, 41, 48, 49, 50, 51, 52, 54, 57, 76, 80, 83, 89, 90, 91, 92, 94, 98, 99, 102, 106, 109, 110, 113, 117, 121, 123, 124, 127, 134, 135, 137, 138, 139, 144, 145, 146, 149, 153, 155, 156, 158
organic, 21, 25, 38, 39, 40, 140

organization, 8, 22, 39, 59, 61, 63, 69, 70, 93, 124, 156, 170
orientation, 32, 34, 93, 140, 141

P

paradigm, xii, xiii, xiv, 2, 156
paradise, 135
participatory, xiv, 73, 85, 155, 166
past, v, xii, xvii, 4, 28, 42, 43, 44, 62, 64, 86, 89, 124, 126, 130, 140, 154, 163
pattern, 14, 20, 22, 23, 42, 90, 98, 100, 103, 106, 132, 169
patternization, 20, 22, 23, 24, 26, 27, 29, 30, 98, 100
Pendentives, 124
performance, 48, 67, 85, 156
phenomenology, xvii, 81, 158
physical, xv, 2, 10, 14, 25, 30, 31, 34, 36, 39, 42, 45, 48, 50, 54, 59, 61, 69, 72, 75, 83, 84, 85, 93, 107, 124, 126, 137, 145, 148, 149, 153
plants, 47, 135, 136, 137
Plato, 92, 112, 128, 164
plurality, 13, 14, 48, 52, 145, 147
positivistic, 7, 78
practical, v, vii, xii, xiii, xvi, xvii, 4, 73, 74, 76, 77, 78, 85, 89, 94, 102, 153, 154, 159, 170
practice, v, vii, xi, xii, xiii, xiv, xvi, xvii, 2, 4, 5, 6, 7, 18, 62, 63, 78, 79, 80, 81, 82, 83, 84, 85, 86, 87, 155, 157, 158, 159, 160, 161, 162, 163, 164, 165, 166, 167, 170
practice movement, xvii, 81, 82, 86
practitioners, vii, xii, 5, 8, 63, 80, 84, 86, 159
pragmatic, 161
principles, v, vii, xi, xii, xiii, xiv, xv, xvi, xvii, xviii, 1, 7, 9, 10, 14, 15, 17, 19, 20, 45, 48, 58, 61, 62, 65, 67, 73, 74, 76, 89, 90, 93, 94, 95, 96, 97, 111, 123, 124, 137, 138, 150, 152, 154, 157, 160, 163, 165
procedural, vii, xi, xiii, xv, 2, 7, 10, 11, 15, 17, 71, 72
process, xiii, xiv, 2, 3, 6, 10, 14, 21, 29, 36, 39, 41, 45, 48, 58, 68, 70, 71, 72, 73, 74, 76, 82, 83, 86, 90, 98, 106, 114, 153, 156, 158, 160, 161, 165
product, xii, xiii, xiv, 2, 102, 153
profession, xii, xiii, xviii, 2
professionals, vii, xi, xii, xvii
public domain, xiv
public space, xii, 31, 32, 33, 95, 150

Q

quantization, 1, 9, 24, 25, 26, 29, 30
Quantum Theory, 24

R

rational, vii, xi, 71, 76, 77, 91, 102
reduction, 7, 170
reflective, 9, 85, 140
repetition, 14, 20, 21, 23, 25, 42, 45, 95, 98, 102, 103, 104, 121, 141
rules, v, vii, xi, xii, xv, xvi, xvii, xviii, 10, 11, 14, 15, 17, 19, 20, 25, 54, 61, 65, 76, 77, 85, 86, 89, 106, 154

S

Safavid, xii, xvi, 114, 119, 126
Safavid dynasty, 114, 119
Saljuqi, 90
Sarai, 141
Sassanid, 90, 113
scientific, vii, xi, 1, 7, 75, 159, 162
semantics, 53, 57, 58, 97

Index

semiology, 53, 56
shadow, 109, 135, 141, 143, 146
Shah mosque, 116, 126, 141, 144, 146
Sheikh Lotfolah mosque, 113, 132, 146
similitude, 42, 44
skylight, 118
square, xii, xvi, 34, 35, 44, 90, 94, 95, 98, 102, 105, 106, 107, 109, 112, 113, 114, 115, 118, 119, 123, 124, 127, 128, 129, 130, 134, 138, 139, 140, 141, 145, 147, 149
Squinches, 124
substantive, vii, xi, xv, xvii, 2, 6, 7, 10, 11, 15, 76, 164
sustainability, xii, xiii, xiv, xvii, 18, 64, 67, 140
sustainable development, xii, xiii, 68, 155, 156, 158
symmetry, 21, 22, 45, 46, 50, 107, 164
synthesis, vii, xii, xiv, 5, 9, 36, 58, 74, 75, 77

T

territories, 31, 32, 33, 34, 62, 63, 139
theory, v, vii, xi, xii, xiii, xiv, xv, xvi, xvii, xviii, 2, 3, 4, 5, 6, 7, 9, 18, 22, 29, 36, 37, 53, 58, 59, 61, 62, 78, 79, 80, 81, 82, 83, 84, 85, 86, 87, 102, 154, 155, 156, 157, 159, 160, 161, 162, 163, 165, 166, 167, 169, 170
theory-practice, xi, 154

Timche, 107, 121, 141
triangle, 45, 68, 112, 125, 147

U

uncertainty, xii, xiii, xiv
unity, 9, 10, 29, 42, 48, 49, 50, 51, 52, 105, 107, 111, 125, 128, 131, 133, 135, 137, 138, 139, 140, 144, 145, 146, 147, 148, 149
urban design, v, vii, xi, xii, xiv, xv, xvi, xviii, 1, 6, 7, 9, 10, 11, 12, 13, 14, 15, 17, 18, 19, 20, 22, 25, 26, 28, 29, 31, 36, 39, 47, 50, 53, 54, 56, 58, 59, 61, 62, 64, 65, 66, 68, 70, 71, 72, 73, 74, 75, 76, 78, 79, 80, 82, 83, 84, 85, 87, 89, 93, 97, 152, 153, 154, 156, 157, 158, 160, 161, 162, 163, 164, 165, 166, 169, 170
urban planning, vii, xi, xii, xiii, xvii, 2, 79, 82, 94, 137, 158, 163, 169
urban space, vii, xi, 11, 12, 13, 14, 15, 69, 76, 89, 94, 102, 146, 156, 157, 158, 162, 163

V

vocabulary, xv, 10, 13, 20, 74, 128

W

water, 67, 84, 133, 134, 138

Related Nova Publications

SWIMMING POOLS: A LANDMARK OF SPRAWL. MEDITERRANEAN URBANITY, LANDSCAPE ARCHITECTURE AND SOCIAL ISSUES

AUTHORS: Luca Salvati, Ph.D. and Ilaria Zambon, Ph.D.

SERIES: Urban Development and Infrastructure

BOOK DESCRIPTION: This book proposes an original interpretation of contemporary metropolitan contexts, candidating residential swimming pools as a landmark of urban sprawl.

HARDCOVER ISBN: 978-1-53614-139-9
RETAIL PRICE: $160

A CLOSER LOOK AT URBAN AREAS

EDITOR: Sahar Romero

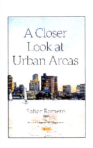

SERIES: Urban Development and Infrastructure

BOOK DESCRIPTION: *A Closer Look at Urban Areas* reviews and analyzes the implementation of the smart city concept applied in recent years in cities of the new Member States.

SOFTCOVER ISBN: 978-1-53614-449-9
RETAIL PRICE: $82

To see a complete list of Nova publications, please visit our website at www.novapublishers.com